THREE WOLVES AT YOUR DOOR

HOW YOU CAN STOP BANKS,
FINANCIAL ADVISORS & GOVERNMENT
FROM DEVOURING YOUR WEALTH

SCOTT ROSS

Library and Archives Canada Cataloguing in Publication

CIP data on file with the National Library and Archives

ISBN (trade paperback) 978-1-55483-629-1
ISBN (ebook) 978-1-55483-630-7

Financial Information Disclaimer

This book is intended for educational and informational purposes only. It is written to help readers better understand how the financial system works, how costs and incentives affect outcomes, and how individuals can make more informed decisions about their money.

Nothing in this book should be considered personal financial, investment, insurance, tax, legal, or accounting advice. Every individual's circumstances are different, and decisions about money should be made with consideration of your own objectives, risk tolerance, and financial situation, ideally in consultation with qualified professionals where appropriate.

The examples and opinions presented reflect the author's experience and perspective at the time of writing. Financial markets, regulations, and tax rules change over time, and no outcome or result is guaranteed.

Reading this book does not create a professional or advisory relationship with the author. Responsibility for financial decisions ultimately rests with the reader.

For Emma and Justin. Watching you become thoughtful, capable adults has been one of my greatest privileges. My hope is that this book helps make your financial future a little clearer, a little fairer, and more firmly in your own hands.

And for every Canadian working to build a better future, you deserve honest information, clear choices, and a system that works for you, not against you.

My deepest thanks to Nathalia, who spent countless hours editing, questioning, and hearing about this project long before it resembled a book. Your steady encouragement was instrumental in bringing it to the finish line.

Contents

Introduction

It might be at a kitchen table, flipping through a statement that looks fine, yet your investment account balances never seem to grow. Or a casual conversation where someone says, confidently, "I don't pay fees—my advisor is free." After years of doing everything right, that uneasy feeling usually has a cause, and it is rarely accidental.

If a stranger reached into your pocket and took $10 out of every $100 you saved, you'd call the police. In our financial system, it's called *standard practice*. Bank interest-rate and currency spreads, layered investment fees, idle cash earning nothing, and embedded product costs each take a bite. Each nibble looks harmless, but the math compounds mercilessly against you. Together, all of this exacts a steady toll on you—a later, leaner retirement, less control of your finances, and fewer choices for your household.

This isn't a conspiracy. It's a system run by three wolves—banks, financial advisors, and government—that puts *their revenues* ahead of your prosperity. Banks focus on market share and maximizing profits from your money. Financial advisors are paid to gather and retain your assets under pay models that reward asset gathering over your outcomes. Governments write the rules and tax your wealth away. The system is not built around your household's best interests. The good news is that once you see and understand the game —the who, the why, and the how—you can flip the odds back in your favour.

Ever since I was a kid in the 1970s, collecting stamps and coins, trading Canadian Tire money for *real* cash, delivering newspapers, and cutting lawns for little old ladies, I have been fascinated by money and how it works. That curiosity eventually became a career in finance, and ultimately, this book.

Free tuition lured me to Military College. The bill arrived later as four years in the Navy, and my first real finance lesson that free usually means *pay later*. Nonetheless, it was a great life experience. Afterward, I earned my MBA at Saint Mary's University, travelled the world for six months, and settled in Vancouver.

I then spent thirty years in the financial industry as a stockbroker, investment advisor, and portfolio manager. Along the way, I learned three enduring lessons. First, education and designations (CFA, CFP, CIM, FCSI, CIPM) are not trophies, but tools that only matter when they are used to improve client outcomes. Second, the financial industry's growth and compensation packages routinely outpace the real economy and the incomes of the households funding it. Third, the system increasingly was, and still is, a scoreboard focused more on making money from you rather than for you. The three wolves may argue otherwise, but the simple truth remains: you keep paying more while they devour an ever-larger piece of your economic pie.

Enough is enough. This book calls out a lopsided system and gives you a roadmap to take back what's yours. It drags the wolves into the spotlight, shows you where your dollars go, and helps you take control deliberately and calmly. It is not a market-history tome or a trading strategy that turns your life into a finance hobby. It is definitely not a get-rich-quick scheme or finfluencer highlight reel. It's a practical, pragmatic, how-to guide containing straightforward steps you can start using immediately.

Throughout this book, you'll follow real-world composite stories—like Jenn's—that reflect what millions of households experience every day. These stories aren't about outsmarting markets; they're about understanding how the system works, and where costs quietly creep in.

By the end, you'll know the game you're in. You'll know how to cut your costs, simplify what you own, and insist on value for the price you pay for advice. Most importantly, you'll measure what actually matters: what you keep, after fees and taxes, at a level of risk you can live with.

How this Book Is Structured

Part I — Meet the Pack: How the Game Really Works

We will meet the wolves and see exactly who is getting rich from your investments. You'll see how your wealth becomes their revenue, why your "all-in" advice cost can amount to thousands of dollars per hour, and run a quick value test to decide if your fees are buying you real outcomes or just expensive promises.

Part II — The Hunt: Tactics the Three Wolves Use to Separate You from Your Money

We decode each wolf's incentive machine in plain English. Banks control product shelves and bury costs in fine print. Financial Advisors follow pay grids that reward custody of your assets, not improvements to your household's results. Government red tape and its unquenchable thirst for your money are a growing menace to your wealth. Learn the specific moves to maximize your success, not theirs.

Part III — Face Your Inner Wolves: Method Over Emotion

The most dangerous wolf is often the one in the mirror. You'll separate myths and noise from method, spot the lies we tell ourselves, and defuse behaviours that quietly, but sometimes very dramatically, eat into your wealth. You'll also learn when to seek advice and on what terms, so that guidance adds value instead of acting like a toll on your portfolio.

Part IV — Tame the Wolves: Build Your Plan and Take Control

Turn insight into action. Design a retirement on your terms, build a plan you can run, and shift from overwhelmed to empowered so you can take back what's yours.

How to Use This Book and the Resource Hub

I'm a firm believer in transparency and truth so this tome is straight-talking by design—meant to put the advantage back on your side. I'll say plainly what works and what doesn't and give credit where credit is due. There are excellent people in finance who help clients every day, but it is also important to know that incentives and structures set prices and policies, and they shape results that aren't always in your best interests.

This book will complement whatever approach you currently use, whether you are a DIY (do-it-yourself) investor, rely solely on an advisor, or are starting fresh. Not everything can fit in these pages, so you will also have access to the Resource Hub, a companion website, with printable checklists, templates, and spreadsheets—all free and easy to access.

The number of titles, designations and acronyms in the financial industry can sometimes make it feel like you are reading an alphabet soup. To help you, this guide also includes a list of the most common financial designations and a glossary of common financial terms and abbreviations.

Bottom Line: This book is about your options. It's about more choices for you, and more control over your time and your future. It is written to help you and designed to pay for itself many times over: whether it's the moment you renegotiate a fee, simplify a structure, or avoid the next poor decision.

Let's start by pulling back the curtain on what "free advice" really costs.

CHAPTER 1

Your Advisor's Payday: Who's Really Getting Rich?

Jenn, a marketing consultant, had just turned 60. After her latest RRSP contribution, plus the recent stock market lift, her account had finally tipped past $1,000,000.

At her favourite Greek restaurant that weekend, she set down the leather-bound menu. "Lisa, did I mention I've got my annual review with Jim on Thursday?"

Her sister glanced up. "Still with Jim at Big Bank?"

"Since the beginning," Jenn replied. "It's already been thirty years." She smoothed the napkin on her lap. "Lately, I've been wondering if I could do better with my investments—if I actually paid attention. Over the years, the kids, work, Mike ... I just haven't made the time."

Lisa nodded, "I get it. It feels complicated until it doesn't." She leaned in. "I've started doing a bit on my own."

Jenn laughed softly. "That's the part I don't get. I can build a marketing plan in a morning. But my investments? Exhausting. Bewildering. Jim handles it all, and … he doesn't charge me anything."

Lisa raised an eyebrow. "Are you sure about *no charge*?"

"I've never had a bill," Jenn responded. "Not once. We don't even talk about costs."

"The accountant in me is fairly certain you're paying," Lisa remarked. "You just don't see it as a single number. I'd suggest you ask him what you paid in dollars over the last twelve months when you see him next."

Jenn stared at the menu but wasn't reading it. "So ... not free."

"Probably not," Lisa said. "But easy to confirm. Just ask."

Jenn smiled and pulled her phone closer. She opened her notes and started typing. "Financial Review: What did I pay last year?"

The following Thursday at 2 p.m., Jenn sat in the noisy bank lobby, waiting for Jim. After several minutes, a smiling, well-dressed young woman greeted her.

"Hello, Jenn! I'm Suzanne, Jim's new associate."

Jenn smiled. "Suzanne, nice to finally put a face to the name!"

Suzanne replied, "I'll take you down to Jim's office now. He's running a bit behind; he's having lunch with new prospective clients. Would you like anything to drink?"

Jenn nodded, "Yes, tea would be wonderful, thank you."

As Jenn waited, she took in Jim's office with its multiple sales awards, family photos, and more than a few snapshots from sunny, sponsor-hosted conferences in beautiful locations. Her thoughts now strayed to how all those perks were paid for, and why, after 30 years as a loyal client, she wasn't the one getting lunch.

Suzanne reappeared with Jenn's tea and a small plate of cookies. Jenn's thoughts returned to the fact that Jim must be doing a great job taking care of her best interests to have such a tastefully adorned office.

Jim popped into the office. "Jenn, so nice to see you again, we haven't talked since last year!"

Jenn looked towards the door, "Yes, hello Jim."

Jim sat down. "Sorry, I'm a bit late, I was meeting new clients for a late lunch." Jim eyed the cookie plate. "Yum, I'm going to dive right into those and then spend a couple of minutes on your portfolio and retirement plans! I'll do my best not to take much of your time."

Jenn smiled, "Sounds good."

They had done this many times, and Jenn was happy with the recent portfolio performance, so the review moved quickly. All that remained was her question about the fees she was supposedly paying.

"Jim, I didn't think there was a fee to manage my RRSP or TFSA, but my sister suggested I ask you if I am paying fees, and if so, how much?"

Jim seemed especially lucid today, more forthcoming than normal. He started talking.

"To keep it simple, let's look only at your RRSP for now. You've been a very diligent saver for the past 30 years, maximizing RRSP contributions and putting in $624,660. (For more details on Jim's calculation please see the Resource Hub, Chapter 1 at www.scottross.ca.) Your account shows about $437,000 in cumulative gains—roughly 4 percent per year on average, and today you have $1,061,475."

Jim elaborated. "There have been good years and bad. I also like to chase and switch funds into the hottest sectors—the tech bubble in 1999, Canadian oil and gas in 2007." Jim winked at Jenn, "And don't tell anyone I'm not a very good market timer, so I never seem to avoid those pesky and inevitable declines that come after chasing short-term, sizzling returns."

Jenn sat up in her chair, "This isn't sounding good, Jim."

"Like I don't know that Jenn," Jim laughed. "Anyway, in recent years, given your age, and to be more *conservative*, I suggested you put your annual contributions into *safe* bond funds. Sadly, when rates jumped in 2022 and 2023, your bond funds were clobbered and your last few years' contributions earned you next to nothing, maybe even lost you money."

Jim continued, "But … ahh ... you should be happy, you're still on the plus side of the ledger, and please know everyone, especially me, makes dumb money mistakes. Also, bank management often tells us what to do with clients' money, but they often get it wrong. I'm just glad it was with your money and not mine!"

Jim's torrent of information was making Jenn's heart beat faster. "And the fees?" she asked.

"Ah, yes," Jim responded. "With your mix of funds, 2 percent per year is bang on."

Jenn looked perplexed. "What do you mean by 2 percent per year?"

Jim stated, "It means you pay 2 percent of the portfolio value I hold for you, each year. Early on, your plan was small, as were the fees you paid, we considered you to be a *C-rated* client, as in *C you later*. Now you're a great client, *A-rated*, since you're paying $20,000 in fees each year. Since we started working together, you've paid approximately $218,000 in fees. Best of all, your fees now cover all the lease costs on my new BMWi7. I love it, it's zero emissions, and my work colleagues are very impressed!"

2% sounds small–until it's $20,000 a year.

Jenn's mouth dropped open. "Pardon me, what the hell are you talking about, Jim? I thought I wasn't paying fees?"

Jim smirked. "That's understandable, I don't normally tell you these things. We do send you paperwork, but it can be very confusing, so you likely never figured it out."

Jim suddenly paused and stared blankly, "You know what, I think Suzanne's baker sprinkled sodium thiopental, or truth serum, in the cookies again. He's not a fan of bank advisors just because one recommended a hot Science and Tech fund at the peak of the Nasdaq bubble in 2000. Legend has it that he lost a ton of money, and now he thinks it's funny when he laces random cookies. It makes me tell the whole truth every now and then."

Jenn tapped Jim's desk with her finger. "Jim, can we please focus on my retirement plan. What about the next ten years for me?"

Jim looked at her. "Thank you for asking, I'm here to help, but honestly, Jenn, I'm not sure, as I've just been more focused on keeping your money here, so we get paid. I will suggest you keep working and make more contributions, since the more money you have here, the more we make. That's why I was late for our meeting today, our biggest raises come from new client money. It's very exciting!"

Jenn exhaled, "I think I'm beginning to see the light."

Jim beamed, "Yes, you are Jenn! Another point, since markets went up 20 percent these past few months, I'll be getting another big raise soon from your increased fees. All that for doing nothing! Markets can be such a wonderful thing for advisors!"

Jim continued, "To answer your question about fees, I think around $255,000 is a reasonable number as to what you will be paying over the next 10 years. It is a lovely round number, and I am pretty sure it will pay for my two boys' university educations."

Jenn sat up straight and was starting to look a bit pale. "Jim, quick math says what I have paid and will pay in the next ten years is more than my husband, Mike, and I paid for our home!"

Jim agreed. "Yeah, that makes total sense. Sadly, for me, you'll probably start paying more attention, look for cheaper options, and maybe even take back more control of your family's finances—and rightfully so—now that your true costs have come to light. We thank you for your business."

Jenn started to tremble, and she felt like a ton of bricks had been dropped onto her chest. She began hyperventilating, unable to enunciate another word, a stinging cold sweat forming across her brow. Suddenly, Jenn felt a warm hand on her shoulder and heard Mike's calming voice.

"Jenn, sweetie ... Jenn … wake up. I think you're having a nightmare."

Out of Sight Out of Mind

Nightmare or not, the fees in Jenn's dream are real. They quietly erode account balances and delay retirement timelines by years.

Imagine if you received an invoice for around $1,700, every month, from your financial institution for vague advice—you'd notice. Yet many people don't, because those fees are deducted silently and out of sight. It's often not the investor's fault; disclosures are confusing, and costs are fragmented.

Being kept in the dark—or dismissing fees as *small*—can cost you tens or even hundreds of thousands of dollars over a lifetime. In Jenn's example, the $218,000 she had paid in fees was not the end of her cost story. Those *hidden fee withdrawals* also reduced her account by another $151,000 due to lost compounding. Together, the fees and lost compounding reduced her account value by a staggering $369,000. While it is not realistic, or even possible, to manage your funds for *free*, minimizing your costs is one of the few levers you fully control to maximize your long-term wealth.

Jenn cannot change the past, but what about the future?

Let's assume she stops contributing to her RRSP for the next ten years, so her total contributions stay at $624,660. Even with no new money added, she will still pay over $255,000 in fees if nothing changes—about 17% more than the $218,000 she paid during the first 30 years, simply because the account is larger.

For Jenn, *better late than never* applies. By acting now to reduce investment costs, she can still save hundreds of thousands of dollars over time. Unfortunately, most investors don't see a single all-in dollar figure for what they pay, which helps explain the persistent belief among many that they pay *nothing*.

Now that we've pulled back the curtain on how fees reduce your returns and on some of the challenges investors face, let's return to Jenn's story and see how she confronts her own financial wake-up call.

Jenn flopped onto the couch like a deflated balloon. "Mike, I'm sorry I'm still in the dumps, but I don't want to go out for dinner tonight. I'm still mortified about the nightmare I had a couple of nights ago." Jenn paused. "I spoke to Lisa this week, and she suggested I become a *do-it-yourself* or *DIY* investor, but honestly, I don't know. I'm not confident about trying to manage our money, and I feel so overwhelmed. I don't even know where to start."

Jenn's husband, a civil engineer at the Department of Transportation, with little interest in day-to-day finances, put down his newspaper with a sigh. "Yeah, I know, sweetheart, and I wish I had more interest in this stuff. I know you only want the best for our family. With the government pension I'll be getting, I've never had to pay attention to this stuff. To be honest, I find the sports pages more appealing."

Jenn frowned. "Really, Mike?"

Mike squirmed in his chair, then sat up. "Oh, that reminds me. Do you remember Scott at the golf club? He worked for the bank for 30 years and retired recently."

Jenn smiled. "Yes, of course I do. You play golf with him every week."

Mike flashed a sheepish grin, "Anyway, over breakfast this morning, I told him how upset you were. He offered to stop by and give us a few insights—a *what's really going on* chat. I invited him for dinner tomorrow night. That, okay?"

"Of course it's okay," Jenn said, her voice a little steadier. "Thank you for doing that Mike. Knowing someone who understands this world and is on our side makes me feel better already."

CHAPTER 2

Meet the Three Wolves: Banks, Financial Advisors, and Government

"Mike, can you grab the door, please?" Jenn called from the kitchen, her hands full of plates.

Mike opened the door and blinked in surprise. "Oh, hi Lisa. I didn't realize you were joining us tonight. You look great! Are you going out on a date later?"

Lisa stepped inside the house and grinned. "Very funny, Mike, and no, I'm not going out on a date, but I did hear we're having dinner with your *friend* from the golf club."

"Apparently," Mike chuckled, as Scott's car pulled into the driveway. Lisa giggled, slipped off her shoes, and headed to the kitchen to find her sister, Jenn.

Scott waved, and Mike headed down the front steps to greet his friend. "Hey Scott, thanks for coming over and offering to help. Jenn's been beside herself, unsure where to start or what to do. She thought our investments were being managed for free, and when she saw the numbers, she nearly lost it."

Scott grimaced knowingly, "Well, that's not a surprise, it's shocking for many when they realize what they are paying in fees."

Just then, Jenn poked her head out the front door. "Hey guys, dinner's ready in five!" she shouted and hurried back to the kitchen. A minute later, Scott and Mike walked into the kitchen and were welcomed by the aroma of Mexican spices and warm corn tortillas.

Lisa shrieked, "Oh, my God, Mike's friend is you!"

Scott gave a sheepish grin. Mike and Jenn looked completely baffled.

Jenn stared at her sister, "Wait, you two know each other?"

Lisa replied, "Yes, we met online and then dated a couple of times, but then COVID happened, the world fell apart, and we lost track of each other. Not much else to say."

Mike laughed and looked at his friend. "Something you want to tell me?"

Before anyone could respond, the oven timer dinged. Jenn hurried to pull a hot skillet of sizzling fajita fixings out of the oven and set it down with a clatter.

Without her usual warm-up, Jenn launched right into an uncharacteristic rant. "I can't believe how much the bank is charging us. They've been taking almost as much as I make from my investments. I've worked my tail off to get ahead and want nothing more to do with them. I'll just do it myself."

"Dear," Mike said carefully, "maybe let's enjoy dinner first?"

Jenn glared at Mike. "Pardon?"

Lisa broke the deafening silence. "Sis, you know I love you to death, but Mike is right. You haven't been yourself since your dream about the bank meeting. Please sit down and take a deep breath. We're all here to help, okay?"

Jenn wiped away a tear from the corner of her eye. "Thanks, Lisa. I'm sorry, everyone, I am just so overwhelmed." She looked toward Scott, "And thank you for coming over to help, Scott."

Scott nodded. "You're welcome, Jenn. This food smells incredible. Why don't we talk about those fees while we eat?"

Jenn took a deep breath and sat down. "Please do, Scott. I think we all need to hear it."

Scott grabbed a small notepad out of his shirt pocket and jotted down a few numbers. "So, here's the quick version. You're not paying a single *fee*—you're feeding three wolves—the Bank, your Financial Advisor, and the Government, and they're now taking an annual $20,000 bite as follows."

Advisor (Jim)	$5,000 (Jim earns $10,000 and pays $5,000 in income tax.)
Bank (Jim's Employer)	$4,000 (The bank receives $10,000, incurs $4,000 in expenses for rent, technology, staffing, etc., leaving $6,000 before paying $2,000 in corporate taxes.)
Other Parties	$2,500 ($4,000 in other expenses rippling outwards, creating $1,500 in various taxes elsewhere.)
Governments	$8,500 (includes $5,000 in income taxes from Jim, $2,000 in corporate taxes from Jim's employer, and $1,500 from Other Parties.)
	Add it all up $5,000 + $4,000 + $2,500 + $8,500 = $20,000

Scott paused and tapped his pen. "So, the bottom line is almost half of your fees end up in government coffers, the rest keeps Jim in BMWs, his employer in fancy lobbies, and everyone else fat and happy—except you. At 2% on $1,000,000 that's not just $20,000 a year—that's also money that won't compound for you. Just remember, percentages are polite, but dollars are honest."

Jenn sat back in her chair, stunned. "I knew it was bad. I just didn't realize ... it was this bad."

Scott looked around, "Have you heard of financial literacy?"

Jenn answered, "Yes, of course."

"Let's take that up a notch to what I call *Wealth Literacy*—think of it as Financial Literacy 2.0," Scott said. "It's your antidote to feeding the three wolves a big slice of your wealth—and you've just taken the first step."

Lisa exhaled. "So, Wealth Literacy is just ... practical financial literacy for investors?"

Scott smiled, "Exactly—and more that they don't teach you: what you really own and who you're really up against, the field you're playing on, and how financial industry incentives work." He cleared his throat and pulled out his phone. "Excuse me, history bomb." He read aloud.

"The national public interest and the interest of investors are adversely affected when investors purchase, pay for ... sell, or surrender securities issued by investment companies without adequate, accurate, and explicit information, fairly presented ... and when investment companies are organized, operated, managed ... in the interest of directors, officers, investment advisors ... or when investment companies are not subjected to adequate independent scrutiny."

Scott looked up. "That's from the U.S. Investment Company Act of 1940, eighty-five years ago. The incentives it warned about are still with us, and relevant to investors on both sides of the border."

Lisa shook her head. "It sounds like a complicit web between the financial services industry, some of their best and brightest, and the government, but somehow nothing has changed in almost a century."

Scott laughed. "You're not wrong. Let me give you a quick example from when I was starting out as a stockbroker in 1993; the latest investment craze was DSC mutual funds."

Jenn raised an eyebrow. "DSC?"

Scott responded, "Sorry, DSC stands for Deferred Sales Charge. Brokers loved them. They got paid a fat 5% upfront commission, and clients thought they loved them too because they didn't see any fees on paper."

Scott continued, "What they didn't realize was that if they tried to pull their money out early, they'd get hit with a nasty 6% redemption penalty. Plus, the broker kept skimming a 0.5% annual *service* fee while they sat on your money. Those funds paid a lot of brokers' rent back in the day. Many jokingly called them *Didn't See that Coming* funds because of the shocking surprise clients would get if they cashed out early."

Lisa didn't look impressed. "Sounds a bit like legalized robbery with a brochure."

Scott agreed. "Yes, to recover those commissions, fund companies charged even heftier management fees, which quietly chewed away at investor returns. Fortunately, DSC funds were banned in 2022, but they still lasted for decades before anybody did something about them."

Jenn exhaled. "So, we're safe from the extra fees now?"

"Not quite. All-in costs haven't fallen much, even after DSCs disappeared," Scott replied.

"Let's look at each of the three wolves in turn—the Bank, the Financial Advisor, and the Government— what they take, how they take it, and how you push back." Scott paused. "First, let's zoom way out, and you can see why your pockets always feel lighter."

Canada From 62 Miles Up

If we look at the financial landscape of Canada from the Karman line, sixty-two miles up at the edge of space, you will see a massive household balance sheet. In mid 2025, households held about $21.6 trillion[1] in assets, or about $500,000 per Canadian. Those assets consisted of things like homes, businesses, cash, and investments of all sorts. We also had debts of $3.2 trillion[2], leaving a net worth of $18.4 trillion[3]. For perspective, picture that as 100 stacks of $20 bills, each stretching over 500 miles into space.

We have a $3.2 trillion[4] economy, half of which goes to household consumption and compensation, while the rest are exports, government spending and capital formation in machinery, equipment, buildings, and houses. The economy produces goods and offers services with about twenty-three million workers.[5] Just over seventeen million are full-time, about four million are part-time and around one and a half million are unemployed.

Your Money on FIRE

In today's economy, it's hard to function without FIRE (Finance, Insurance, and Real Estate). Banks, brokerages, insurers, mortgage lenders, and real estate agents have all built incentives to *encourage* you to keep your money moving by trading, borrowing, insuring, refinancing, and renewing. Every move throws off fees, commissions, interest, premiums, and taxes. All that activity feels normal because the system is designed to make it feel normal.

Canadian banks employ[6] over 300,000 people in Canada and over 400,000 worldwide. Insurers employ over 400,000[7] across more than three hundred companies in the life, health, property, and casualty insurance areas. Add thousands more at investment dealers, asset managers and other financial services, and you have about 4.0% of the Canadian workforce. That is the first wolf, the Bank wolf, the financial system that takes a slice every time your money moves.

The Bank Wolf: The World's Greatest Skimming Machine

"The mutual fund industry is, indeed, the world's largest skimming operation ... a trough from which fund managers, brokers, and other insiders are steadily siphoning off an excessive slice of the nation's household, college, and retirement savings."
—U.S. Senator Peter Fitzgerald, 2004

Senator Fitzgerald was describing the United States, but the pattern is also familiar in Canada in 2025, where the mutual fund industry manages over $2 trillion in over 3,000 different funds. There are also many hundreds of billions tied up in over 1,000 ETFs (Exchange Traded Funds), fee-based programs and pension plans. Despite technological advancements, soaring productivity, and decades of public scrutiny, the skimming has accelerated, not slowed, as industry profits have exploded at a much faster rate than both the economy as a whole and the financial wealth of Canadians.

For example, in a September 26, 2024, report, the Investment Funds Institute of Canada (IFIC) proudly announced "The investment funds industry's GDP grew by an extraordinary 82 percent between 2012 and 2023, compared with 23 percent for the Canadian economy overall. In addition, the industry achieved large productivity gains over the past decade, driven by technology and innovation. This is during a period when there has been an overall flattening of productivity across all industries. Wages in the investment industry increased by 46 percent, compared to 35 percent across all industries."

The salient point that IFIC did not share in their release was that *industry GDP* is drawn from your investment accounts. The financial services industry passed little of its productivity benefits to you via lower management fees, resulting in profit margins that continue to make most other industries blush. While the financial industry celebrated record-breaking results, you kept paying the bills as more and more of your dollars continued to be siphoned away. To do that, they also needed help from the second wolf.

The Financial Advisor Wolf: The Business of Advice

Have you ever wondered why financial advice appears everywhere but is still expensive? You are right, it isn't scarce, but it is lucrative, and the system is absolutely packed with people getting rich from your savings. Canada's main financial watchdog—the Canadian Investment Regulatory Organization (CIRO)—oversees about 110,000 registered advisors across the country. There are also advisors at a myriad of other financial institutions, such as credit unions, insurance companies of all sorts, and independent financial firms, who can provide you with financial and investment advice.

Among them, around 10,000 advisors work at big bank-owned brokerages, where they are often among the highest-paid employees in the industry. Unless your advisor is a new hire, part-time, or particularly bad at their job, they're earning at least $500,000 a year—comfortably placing them in the top 0.5% of Canadian income earners.

It doesn't stop at advisors. The investment, pension, and banking industries also include thousands of executives, fund managers, hedge fund operators, and private equity managers earning $1 million or more per year. We often imagine that it is CEOs, star athletes, doctors, or entrepreneurs who dominate the ranks of Canada's highest earners. The reality is that finance quietly fills a large portion of the ranks of the country's highest earners, all earned from your money—year after year.

Why Are There So Many People Offering Financial Advice?

Today, there is a financial advice giver for about every 100 households of the approximately 15 million households in Canada. For comparison, Canada has approximately 90,000 doctors (some 50,000 are GPs), 210,000 accountants and 27,000 dentists.

If we assume each advisor very generously spent 10 hours per household each year, that would be 1000 hours of advisory time, or barely part-time work if we compare that to a typical 35-hour work week, which equals 1,750 hours per year. There would still be plenty of time for advisors to play golf, ski and go on vacations, yet a large portion of households get little or no ongoing, objective advice. Why?

The modern advisor model rewards asset gathering and product placement, not continuous, unconflicted guidance. Financial advice today isn't built to help you win, but to extract more dollars from what you own. It's a high-pressure sales tournament—a beauty pageant of products, hype, and hustle to capture assets that often soak up a disproportionate amount of an advisor's time.

The business model? Sell something. Move on. Find richer clients. Repeat.

Ready for wolf number 3?

The Government Wolf

Nearly every financial product you touch—whether it's a savings account, an RRSP, or a mutual fund—quietly feeds enormous tax revenues into government coffers. Somehow, almost all of it flies comfortably under the public's radar.

In 2023, Members of Parliament lined up to publicly scold the big grocery chains—Loblaws, Metro, Sobeys, Costco, and Walmart—for *excess profits*. These five companies control about 80% of the Canadian grocery market and collectively made $6 billion in profit in 2023.

Fast forward to 2024, and the largest grocer, Loblaws, netted $2.17 billion[8] in after-tax profits on $61.0 billion[9] in sales, about a 5% increase over 2023 and a 3.5% profit margin. Sounds big, right?

Compare that to RBC, Canada's largest bank, which brought in nearly identical revenue—$57.5 billion[10] in 2024—but turned it into a staggering $16.2 billion[11] in profit. That is a 28.2% profit margin after taxes, or more than 8 times that of Loblaws.

For the calendar year 2025, it is estimated Loblaws will increase its sales by approximately 7 percent to $65 billion, earn about 12% more or $2.4 billion, and pay around $800 million in income tax. Now what about the Big 6 banks? (Author's Hint: They had a very good year!)

Given the October fiscal year end for Canadian banks, we know that RBC earned $20.4[12] billion on $66.6 billion[13] in revenues in 2025. That is a 16 percent revenue increase and a whopping 26 percent profit increase. Overall, the Big 6 banks (RY, TD, Bank of Nova Scotia, BMO, CIBC and National), earned $63 billion[14] in 2025, or about $1,500 for every man, woman and child in Canada. This is *after* paying out over $25 billion in various taxes (another $600 for each person in Canada).

Translation: Over $2,000 in *profits and taxes* per person to the Big 6 alone—quite a fistful of cash for the average household.

The result? Crickets. No performative outrage. No political hearings. No front-page condemnations.

Here's another fun, but sad, fact: the banks and insurance companies bring in far more revenues than Canadians spend on groceries or new home construction. So, who really keeps Ottawa's lights on?

The Golden Goose

It's no exaggeration to say that the government adores the financial services industry. It's not just laying golden eggs—it's laying golden taxes every year. Banks, insurers, and investment firms generate massive streams of corporate taxes, payroll taxes, GST, HST, special bank levies, and income taxes from their highly paid employees. Let's take a look.

The First Golden Egg: **Corporate Taxes.** In the November 2025 Canada Strong Budget 2025[15] document, the 2024-2025 federal government forecast for corporate income tax was $97 billion. The Big 6 banks alone contributed around one-quarter of that total, paying over $20 billion in corporate, payroll and sales taxes. Many more billions came from the hundreds of other financial and insurance companies.

The Second Golden Egg: Paychecks. In the same November 2025 budget document, the government forecast $234.3 billion in personal income tax. At the Big Six banks alone, salaries, bonuses, and benefits were almost $80 billion, heavily concentrated with many employees in the top marginal tax brackets. To be conservative, this would generate a tax haul of at least $20 billion. Count in the billions more paid out at hundreds of other companies, including insurers and investment firms, it is no wonder Ottawa loves every financial industry paystub!

The Third Golden Egg: Dividends. In 2025, the financial industry paid roughly $40 billion in dividends ($30 billion from the Big Six Banks). So, what happens to those dividend payments when you receive them? They are taxed again! Whether you receive dividends directly, through a mutual fund or ETF, or ultimately as payments from a registered plan, the government gorges again.

Even More Golden Eggs: Canadian investors also pay taxes on dividends from other companies, interest earned, and capital gains from all sources. Even when you shelter your investments inside RRSPs, pensions or similar plans, the government patiently waits. Once you start making withdrawals, or die, they tax the full amount withdrawn. This includes those decades of original contributions, but even more onerously, all the investment growth comprised of interest, dividends and capital gains from your plan's holdings.

Still not enough? Depending on where you live, GST or HST also applies to investment management services, meaning you pay an extra 5% to 15% for the privilege. For example, the Investment Funds Institute of Canada (IFIC) recently noted that its members generated over $40 billion (approximately 1.3% of the country's $3.2 trillion economy) in revenues. Much of that haul was taxed again with GST or HST, depending on where you live, quietly adding another $3 billion or more to government coffers.

In other words, you are not just paying for a service; you are also paying sales taxes on the act of being skimmed. If the government really wanted to help Canadians save for retirement, one easy fix would be to make investment management fees GST/HST exempt.

Add it all up, and you have around 4% of Canada's workforce delivering a disproportionate slice of every tax bucket. The cycle hums, enriching the bank and insurance sectors, their employees, and governments hooked on the revenue.

So where does that leave investors like Jenn and you? Paying the bills, fees, and taxes—now and later—in a system that isn't broken but working as designed. No wonder retirement feels uphill for so many.

"I love the giant skimming-machine analogy," Jenn noted, shaking her head. "It shows how much of our money gets siphoned off by the industry and the government and just how many bites the Government wolf takes out of the same dollars."

"Agreed," Scott replied. "It's a lot to take in, but a necessary step to knowing what you are up against. Many will argue that without our bloated financial sector, our economy will suffer. Not so. Other industries would expand to fill the gap and keep more of what they earn instead of paying out excessive banking costs. Consumers would keep more in their pockets, *hidden* taxation would shrink, and the country would be wealthier with less money squandered in Ottawa, the provincial capitals, or Jim's next car."

Scott added, "Yes, we need a stable financial system, but that's not an excuse for predatory pricing and the inflated fees Canadians are stuck paying."

Mike responded, "So, if I've got this right, we pay so much because we have an overbuilt financial industry filled with overcompensated advisors, and a government shackled to the Golden Goose with no incentive to change."

Scott agreed, "That sounds about right!"

Mike looked at Jenn. "Dear, I think our first step this week is to talk to our advisor, Jim, find out exactly what we are paying in each account, in dollars, and write it down. I think I finally get Scott's point about percentages. They sound harmless, but in dollars … ouch."

Scott sat forward. "I'd say that nails it! Now that you know what you're paying and who gets it, we'll zoom in on the costs of the different investment products and services you use."

Lisa winked at Scott. "Let's hear all about it, Scott—after Mike cuts the pie."

CHAPTER 3

Inside the Fee Maze: How Your Money Turns Into Their Profits

Mike carefully sliced generous pieces of cherry pie, giving Jenn an encouraging nod as he handed her a plate. He was glad to see his wife back to her levelheaded self.

Jenn tapped her fork. "Okay, now we know where the money goes. What are the actual costs?"

Scott, trying to grin around a forkful of pie, said, "Happy to, but this is the part where most people start to squirm."

Mike looked up from his dessert. "Is this the part where we find out we're paying three times without realizing it?"

"In fairness, it's not exactly three times, but it's definitely more than once," Scott replied. "Management expense ratios, advice fees, trading commissions, embedded trailer fees—it's a buffet of quiet deductions. And the worst part? Most people have little idea of everything they're paying for."

Lisa raised an eyebrow. "Is this even legal?"

Scott looked up with a thin smile. "Legal? Yes. Transparent? That depends on your definition. Regulators have allowed these structures, but the disclosures are often buried in voluminous and dense paperwork. I was recently flipping through a couple of 2025 simplified prospectuses from *Big Bank Asset Managements*, one was 377 pages[16] long, and the other was 396 pages[17], both with tiny print. Good luck finding what you need in there."

Jenn's dinner was starting to churn in her stomach, but curiosity outweighed the queasiness. "Please walk us through the details on how the three wolves are devouring our money?"

Scott agreed, "Well, let's start with the basics."

The Fee Maze—What You're Really Paying (and Why It Matters)

As markets and technologies have advanced, countless clever players have introduced new investment products and solutions, often with more convoluted, opaque and expensive cost structures. In addition, some advisors or planners may not give you the whole picture of what you are really paying, as their incentives to keep your assets under their management may not align with your desire for full transparency on costs.

Today, the main fee models, from most to least common, are:

1. Fees on Assets Under Management (AUM) or Assets Under Administration (AUA)
2. Brokerage Commissions
3. Advice-Only
4. Performance Fees

1. Fees on Assets Under Management (AUM) or Assets Under Administration (AUA)

Under this model, you pay a percentage of your account value each year to the management firm, regardless of whether your investments perform well or poorly. In the last two decades, it has become the go-to model because it generates a steady, low-effort, and hefty revenue stream for the industry. Despite massive improvements in technology that have slashed the costs of managing money, fees charged to customers haven't gone down accordingly. In fact, fees today are usually much higher than they were many decades ago when managing a portfolio was far more labour-intensive and without the benefit of advanced portfolio management software. (Translation: more revenue for them, less value and transparency for you.)

Scott took a sip of his drink. "You've probably heard the term *management fee* or *M.E.R.*, that's short for Management Expense Ratio (M.E.R.). It covers management, legal, marketing, and administrative costs, but usually doesn't include trading costs. Those show up as the Trading Expense Ratio or T.E.R."

Jenn acknowledged, "Yes, but I don't really pay attention to them. Why should I care?"

Scott grimaced. "Here's why. For you, they are thousands of dollars per year leaking out of your pot of money!"

Mike sat up. "How?"

Scott replied, "Take a well-known Canadian equity fund that's been around for over 30 years. The fund charges a 2.25% management fee; it averages about 0.40% in other expenses and 0.15% in trading costs for an effective all-in fee of 2.80% (2.25+0.40+0.15= 2.8%). Add 13% HST, and the total comes to 3.16%."

Mike commented, "In English, please?"

Scott stated, "It means for every $100,000 you have invested in that fund, you are being charged $3,160 per year in fees and taxes."

Jenn stared at the page. "That's … astounding. How much would we pay over 25 years?" (For more details on this calculation and others in this chapter, please see the Resource Hub, Chapter 3 at www.scottross.ca.)

Scott picked up his calculator. "Okay, assuming the fund earned 6% before fees, subtract the management fee and taxes of 3.16% and you net 2.84% per year. After 25 years, $100,000 becomes around $201,000."

Lisa remarked, "That doesn't seem all that bad, you doubled your money."

Scott looked up from his calculator again. "Well, without fees, your $100,000 would grow to about $429,000 for a gain of $329,000. That's $228,000 more in your pocket."

Lisa's mouth fell open. "That's unbelievable!"

Scott added. "We know it's not realistic to think you can have your money managed for free, but you can minimize your management fees—and it likely won't be with a traditional AUM advisor or at the bank."

Mike asked Scott, "What if we get our costs down to 0.5%. What would that do to your example."

Scott responded, "Give me a few seconds. So, with a 0.5% fee, you would end up with $381,339 from your original $100,000 for a net increase of $281,339."

Lisa grinned, "Well, the accountant in me says that $281,339 is almost three times the return of the $101,396 net increase from the high fee example!"

Scott smiled. "Yes, let that sink in for a minute. It can easily be the difference between a great retirement and no retirement. I sometimes joke that M.E.R. really stands for *Making Everyone Rich but You.* Let's move on to the other fees and costs investors incur."

Mutual fund fees (AUM or AUA) range from 1% to 3%. This means you'll pay $1,000 to $3,000 per year per $100,000 invested.

Another rapidly growing option is the Exchange Traded Fund (ETF), a managed fund that trades like a stock. The ETF market has exploded in recent years, and its size and depth are now starting to rival that of the mutual fund industry. ETFs tend to be cheaper, but don't get fooled: lower cost doesn't mean no cost.

ETF fees range from 0.04% to 1% ($40 to $1,000 per year per $100,000 invested).

Caution: Some advisors may buy ETFs to put inside your fee-based account. This will add an additional 0.5% to 2.0% advisory fee on top, bringing your total cost to as high as 2.5% ($2,500 per year per $100,000 invested). For comparison, a do-it-yourself (DIY) investor can buy ETFs at a discount brokerage for less than $10 per trade and skip the ongoing advisor fees entirely.

A third, quietly expanding choice is the proprietary, fee-based *solution*—often branded with names like SMA (Separately Managed Account), UMA (Unified Managed Account), investment platforms, or wrap accounts. These are pre-built, low-maintenance packages sold as custom solutions. They're a win for your advisor (less work, more margin) and a loss for you (higher fees, lower transparency).

SMA/UMA fees range from 1% to 3% ($1,000 to $3,000 per year per $100,000 invested).

Many of these solutions also bundle in mutual funds or ETFs, meaning you're paying for both the wrap fee and any investment costs inside the wrap.

2a. Full-Service Brokerage Commissions

In this model, you pay a commission each time a transaction, such as buying or selling a stock, bond, or ETF, occurs in exchange for personalized advice and order execution. One upside to this model is the commission costs are itemized, so you will see the cost in black and white on your trade confirmation slips.

The problem? This model rewards activity, not quality advice. Historically, many brokers perfected the art of the sales story and were great at motivating clients to buy and sell, often more than necessary. This excess activity was called *churning*, and regulators and clients eventually caught on. Money management should be boring, but this model makes it feel like a casino with lots of activity, the stress to match, and you end up leaving more of your money on the table.

Jenn sighed, "So, in this game, the house always wins?"

Scott elaborated, "Yes, but unlike Vegas, they don't serve you free drinks while they're taking your money."

In the 20th century, this was how brokers made their living. With the rise of discount brokerages and fee-based models, this old model has mostly faded away. In hindsight, this model was actually more transparent than today's layered AUM models and could also be significantly less expensive over the longer term if you had a good advisor whose interests aligned with yours.

Full-service brokerage commissions can range from $125 to thousands of dollars per trade. Bond and GIC commissions are generally in the 0.25% to 1% range, but these are often hidden or built into the price you pay. Always ask your advisor what commission is baked into the trade cost—you might be surprised.

2b. Discount Brokerage Commissions

Discount brokerages offer far lower commissions than traditional full-service firms, but you don't receive advice, and you execute the trades yourself. In many cases, these trades appear *free*, but these free trades usually mean the brokerage is making money via pricing or currency exchange spreads. Depending on your trading volume, these spreads might quietly cost you more than an old-fashioned commission. Remember, there's still no such thing as a *free lunch,* just a cleverly bundled trade confirmation.

Bond and GIC trading through discount brokerages is often underwhelming given the limited inventory, lack of advice, and the fact that costs can mirror those of full-service brokers.

Discount brokerage commissions typically range from $0 to under $30 per transaction. Depending on your activity level, you might pay less than 0.1% annually—or about $100 per

$100,000—with no ongoing fees. Like full-service brokerages, fixed income, bond and GIC commissions are generally in the 0.25% to 1% range.

2c. Initial Public Offerings (IPOs) and Secondary Issues

IPOs and secondary issues (securities already trading in the market) generally don't show the commission to the buyer, but that does not mean it is free, as these embedded commissions are often in the 1.5% to 3.0% range and ultimately will increase the price of the security you are buying.

The issuing company pays the fee behind the scenes, and your advisor and brokerage firm share the commission. While some IPOs are solid investments, others are just well-marketed opportunities to stoke excitement and generate more commissions through subsequent transactions.

3. Advice-Only

In this model, your advisor charges a set hourly or engagement rate and may offer financial planning or coaching. They should not be collecting commissions or percentage-based management fees. This model has the potential to become the *Future of Advice*, placing client interests first, and avoiding the conflicts that plague commission-driven or fee-based services. This delivery format could help the investment industry function more like a real profession—on par with accounting, law, or engineering.

Jenn leaned forward. "So, you mean I could just hire someone for advice without having to hand over my portfolio?"

Scott agreed, "Exactly. You pay for their brain, not for them to babysit your money."

Scott added, "And unlike some other models, there's no incentive for them to keep your money parked where it benefits them most."

Jenn paused and re-examined the fee examples Scott had prepared earlier. "The cost savings could be massive over time. So why doesn't everyone do this?"

Scott replied, "With the advice-only model, the bill comes directly to you. You see it and touch it, so it may feel expensive. The irony, in almost all cases, is it will be a fraction of what you would be paying in AUM models, where the fees are quietly compounding against you in the background. Remember out of sight, out of mind?"

Scott set down his pen. "And here is the kicker—when I was an advisor, I couldn't even offer a fee for advice model. Most financial firms and their compensation structures require that client assets be *on the books* so they can collect either commissions or AUM/AUA fees. Advice-only doesn't fit that mould, so it's rarely, if ever, offered by the big players even though that is all that most people really need."

Typical advisory fees range from $150 to $500 per hour, but always ask if the professional receives any other compensation (e.g., referral fees) from third parties that could influence their recommendations.

4. Performance Fees

This fee structure rewards investment managers and advisors for generating *excess* returns, usually in hedge funds or private equity funds. Excess returns are measured against a benchmark (like the S&P 500 or TSX 60) or a specified target return. While it might align incentives on paper, in practice, the manager shares in your upside but not your downside, which may lead to them taking outsized risks with your money. These structures have become increasingly common and more complex, which is not necessarily a good thing. If you venture into this space, bring a good flashlight and maybe even a helmet.

Fees typically start at around 2% of AUM but can balloon quickly. A common setup is *2 and 20:* a 2% base fee, plus 20% of any returns above a set threshold or hurdle rate. For example, if your returns beat the hurdle rate by 10%, you would pay 4% in

fees. This would be composed of a 2% performance fee (0.2% X 10%) in addition to the regular 2% management fee. Always read the fine print if you are presented with one of these *opportunities* and be exceptionally skeptical as to why. (Translation: Your Advisor knows they can earn a potentially higher fee from these structures.)

The Dreaded Double Dip

One particularly problematic practice is the *double dip*, when an advisor charges both a mutual fund trailer fee and an added AUM fee on the same assets. Sometimes the duplicate costs are hidden inside the product itself, making it feel like a free lunch, but only for the advisor.

Impact: This may result in an extra 0.5% to 1.0% in the fees you are paying annually ($500 to $1,000 per $100,000 invested), resulting in a lower net return to you.

The Biggest Dip

Most of us are fine with a junior associate handling part of the service we pay for, such as in law or accounting, but at a discounted rate with proper oversight and quality control. Similarly, investment advisors and financial planners will often have other *team members* that may be doing a large part, if not all, of the work on your accounts while they are busy with other activities.

The catch? Even though these junior team members are less qualified and earn significantly less than your advisor, you still get charged the same full percentage fee on every dollar.

This Biggest Dip is not an *oversight* but a deliberate business model that allows your advisor to scale up their compensation while scaling down their effort. Ironically, the more successful your advisor appears, the higher the probability you are paying premium prices for less personal attention.

Jenn set down her fork and glanced around the table. "From now on, we need to price everything all-in—management fees, total M.E.R., trading expenses and any added advice or performance fees."

Mike chimed in, "And no double-dips. If there's a wrap outside and fund fees inside, or trailers plus an advice charge, we walk. We'll also pay attention to who's really doing the work on our portfolio so we're not paying senior-level fees for junior-level execution."

Scott glanced around the table. "Bottom line: price it all in dollars and realize you're buying someone else's revenue model. That's how you turn the maze back into a straight line."

Scott tapped the folder. "Next, let's see whether those dollars buy real value—or just deliver expensive promises."

Mike slid the half-full pie plate back across the table and topped up Jenn's slice. Forks clinked; the room eased. Scott tapped the folder and smiled. "Dessert again, then value. Let's map what you really get and what it costs."

CHAPTER 4

Costs Without Value: The Price of Expensive Promises

Suddenly, Jenn slipped back into the nightmare where her financial planner, Jim, stood grinning as he joked about paying for his sons' education with the fees she was handing over from her RRSP.

"It still makes me so angry, thinking of what our family could have done with the savings from just that one account. My trust in the system has been shattered, and I feel ripped off."

Scott agreed. "Trust me, I get it. When I worked at the bank, advisors had to keep their own and immediate family accounts with the firm. Even with an employee discount, the fees bothered me. After I retired, I simply moved my accounts to the bank's discount brokerage arm. It only took two days, nothing in my accounts changed, and now I'm saving thousands of dollars per year."

"And here is a little secret," he shared. "In many cases, the bank's full and discount brokerages use much of the same back-office infrastructure, so you still have the security of your preferred bank as your assets are custodied in the same place, just at a fraction of the cost! Your broker or advisor won't tell you this."

Lisa raised an eyebrow, "So, what's a fair price?"

Scott replied, "Great question. A fair price means paying an amount proportionate to the value received; nothing more, nothing less."

Mike, Jenn, and Lisa all nodded in agreement. "No surprises

there," said Jenn.

Scott said, "Don't beat yourselves up for trusting the system and not seeing what was hidden from you. The financial services industry has thrived on a lack of transparency."

Jenn leaned forward. "Okay, so can you explain to us what value we're really getting for these fees?"

Scott responded, "Absolutely. I'll also cover the other services that support your whole wealth picture. Some roles earn their keep; others don't. Let's name each role and put a price tag and a value beside it."

Your Wealth Dream Team—Price Tags Attached

Your wealth team typically covers five major areas: legal, tax, insurance, financial planning, and investment management. Let's examine what each usually costs and the value you get in return.

Lawyers usually charge hourly for time spent, and their pricing is generally transparent. Novice lawyers may charge $150 to $250 per hour. Mid-level hourly rates are often in the $250 to $450 range, while veteran and specialist lawyers may charge $450 to $1,000+ per hour. An estate package including your will, power of attorney and health representation typically costs $500 to $2,000, depending upon complexity.

Accountants are your go-to for significant tax work and business advice. In some cases, they can do an excellent job providing general financial planning services as well. Similar to lawyers, fees range widely, roughly $100 to $800+ per hour, depending on their experience and the scope of work. A personal tax return might cost you $200 to over $2,000 per year, depending on complexity.

Insurance advisors usually get paid commissions embedded in the premiums you pay. For example, a car insurance renewal might have embedded commissions in the $50 to $300 range on average. However, life-insurance commissions can be large. Depending on coverage amount, age, and annual premium, commissions are often thousands of dollars, and in rarer cases, well over $100,000, even with an occasional $1 million-plus commission.

Financial Planners typically charge $150 to $500 per hour, similar to an accountant's rate. A comprehensive financial plan usually runs $1,000 to $4,000 for most households. Premium plans priced at $10,000+ are usually only justified if you own multiple businesses or have complex cross-border holdings.

Planners often recommend annual updates, but for most people, a refresh every 4 to 7 years—or after a major life event such as a marriage, divorce, birth, death, large windfall, or retirement, is more than enough. Think of it like a medical check-up: useful for catching problems and setting a baseline, but it doesn't replace regular exercise. If you overspend or ignore common-sense habits, even the best plan won't save you. The real value comes from the planning process and your ongoing decisions, not from a binder that gathers dust in a drawer.

Investment Advice and Management usually entails being charged a percentage of your assets under management (AUM), commonly 0.5% to 2% annually. On $500,000, that's $2,500 to $10,000 per year. Some retail mutual funds push total costs toward 3%

($15,000 per year).

With investment advice, three factors make it harder to judge value: M.E.R.s and other related fees are often not fully disclosed, charges aren't presented as an hourly equivalent, and account balances fluctuate with markets. Depending on portfolio size, what you pay can effectively amount to thousands of dollars per hour for the actual service time you receive.

The All-Inclusive Problem

Bundled pricing in finance works a lot like a typical Mexican all-inclusive vacation. You pay one price for your hotel, food, drinks, and entertainment—whether you use them or not. In financial services, the *all-inclusive* bundle often includes both investment management and financial planning, often by the same person or team. The trouble? It is difficult to discern what each part really costs and the value it adds.

Job titles make this even murkier. The industry offers a dizzying mix of roles—Investment Advisor, Financial Planner, Financial Advisor, Portfolio Manager, Wealth Manager, Investment Specialist, and dozens more. Some will reflect real distinctions in education, licensing, or firm structure, but many are simply marketing titles and have little to do with the actual scope or quality of service. For further clarification, refer to the listing of common designations after Chapter 21.

Whichever title you come across, keep in mind that services land in one of two categories: planning activities or investing advice. We will use these two simple definitions going forward.

Planner: Focuses on creating or updating a financial plan with typical services such as retirement projections, budgeting, tax strategies, and insurance recommendations.

Advisor: Focuses on investment-related services to include portfolio design, trade execution, monitoring performance, and providing investment recommendations.

Scott leaned back. "Okay, want a quick history lesson on that *All-Inclusive* problem?"

Mike asked, "Do we have a choice?" Everyone laughed. "Fire away!"

Scott grinned. "Back in the day, investment advisors, and the stockbrokers before them, were like financial royalty. They were very well paid with high fees and commissions to custody, administer, trade, and manage your assets."

Lisa remarked, "Sounds like a nice gig."

"Oh, it was," Scott noted. "And before the 1960s, nobody cared about financial planning because retirement was short. You stopped working, you got a gold watch, you ... well, you didn't need much of a plan."

Jenn quipped. "Cheery thought."

"Then, by the 1990s," Scott continued, "people were living longer on average, defined benefit pension plans were disappearing, and so financial planning became a real thing. The Financial Planners Standards Council popped up in 1995 and set standards for the industry (now part of FP Canada). However, before long, the planners realized, 'Hey, we can give investment advice too.' That's when the *double-dipping* into your pot of money started. Charge for the plan and then quietly charge again to manage your assets."

Mike raised an eyebrow. "And advisors just let that slide?"

Scott laughed. "Not a chance. When advisors saw the planners multiplying, they added planning to their own services to protect their turf and keep clients from wandering off. And just like that, you've got planners doing advisor stuff, and advisors doing planner stuff ... like everyone swapped jerseys mid-game without telling the fans."

Jenn shook her head. "So, who's actually winning this game—us, or them?"

Scott chuckled. "Oh, that's easy. Almost aways them, but we're going to see what we can do about that for you." He leaned in. "Remember what that low-cost baseline or reference portfolio looks like?"

Lisa sat up and put up her hand, "Oh, I do!"

Scott replied, "Well, once you see the floor, it's a lot harder for someone to sell you the ceiling."

Use ETFs as a Benchmark

Fortunately, exchange-traded funds (ETFs) give us something the financial industry has rarely offered—full transparency. They make it easy to see exactly what you are paying for and provide a clear-cut baseline to compare the price you pay to the value you receive.

A low-cost, diversified portfolio can be built using ETFs for 10 to 30 basis points or 0.1% to 0.3%. This equates to $100 to $300 per year per $100,000 invested. Compare that to the typical retail mutual fund, which charges around 2% (200 basis points) or $2,000 per $100,000 per year.

Another useful yardstick is what professional and institutional investors pay for active money management in products like wrap programs or investment pools. They often charge 5 to 50 basis points ($50 to $500 per $100,000) for underlying management, but then your advisor or planner will likely add on an *account management fee* of another 0.5% to 1.5% ($500 to $1,500 per $100,000) for custody, advice, oversight and administration.

Here is a real-world example. I still hold investment funds through my former employer's group savings plan at one of Canada's leading insurance companies. One of the funds is an extremely popular bank mutual fund, costing me 0.25% in management fees. If you or I walk into a branch of that same bank and buy a retail series of the same fund, the fee jumps to 2.1% or more than eight times higher for the same manager and strategy.

Jenn Wants Answers

Jenn could no longer sit quietly. "So what value am I really getting in my RRSP account?"

"Well, in your RRSP you're paying $20,000 a year," Scott noted.

"I'd say the value you're getting is about $2,500 for investment management, a financial plan every 4 years or about $500 per year, and two hours of review time each year, let's call it $500. A total value of around $3,500 ($2,500 + $500 + $500)."

Jenn fixed Scott with a cold stare, "$3,500—that's it?"

Scott stated, "Hey, I'm just the messenger, but since you put it that way, yes, for this year's delivered work."

Mike exhaled sharply. Lisa's mouth dropped open.

Scott paused, "To add insult to injury, if you back out the $2,500 value of your investment management, you are effectively paying $17,500 ($20,000 - $2,500) for the other services and about four hours of advice."

Jenn leaned forward, "And?"

Scott winced, "It means you are effectively paying four thousand, three hundred and seventy-five dollars per hour ($17,500 ÷ 4 = $4,375) to your advisor. Kind of like paying expensive champagne prices for tap water."

Mike blinked several times. "That's more than a Bay Street lawyer, brain surgeon, and luxury car mechanic combined."

"Yep," Scott said flatly. "I have seen instances where people believed they were getting *free* financial advice but were effectively paying over $10,000 per hour. Makes everything else in life look like a bargain."

Jenn turned to Mike. "Honey, if I understand what Scott has shown us, we should be able to trim our overall annual investment and planning costs by $15,000 or more by making a few adjustments."

Jenn looked at Scott, "Is that correct?"

"Yes," Scott responded. "That's a reasonable conclusion, and that is just in your RRSP."

Jenn stood up, energized. "And for planning activities, we could hire an advice-only financial planner when needed. For tax preparation, or when Mike and I redo our wills and estate plans this year, we simply pay our accountant and lawyer directly, as needed. I also see that my financial planner, while he sometimes touched on these topics in our annual reviews, didn't bring any real value because he's not qualified to do any work in these areas. Am I on the right track here?"

"Exactly!" Scott agreed. "You're a great student. You now know what you are paying, where the money is going, and what you are getting in return."

Mike, Jenn, and Lisa exhaled, each smiling as though giant weights had finally been lifted from their shoulders.

Jenn smiled at Scott, "Thank you for breaking the system down in plain English for us. I'm liking this wealth literacy thing, especially now that I know the price tag on every team member."

Scott chuckled and stood up. "Happy to help. Why don't we meet next week and talk more about the Bank Wolf? We'll put the spotlight on the financial industry and why *beating the market* usually beats you, why chasing the Holy Grail of Investing may be fruitless, and the sales machine that sells it all."

Jenn and Lisa nodded, "Works for us!"

CHAPTER 5

The Performance Mirage: Why *Beating the Market* Beats You

Scott knocked on the door. Jenn opened it, and Lisa waved from the kitchen island.

Scott smiled, “Good morning, ladies. Ready for some investment insights today?”

“For sure,” Jenn replied. “Mike’s golfing today, so it’s just us.”

Lisa said, “We both did some web surfing this week and couldn’t believe how much information there is on investing and how easy it seems to *beat the market*.”

Scott chuckled. “Sounds great, but what exactly are you talking about?”

“It seems like everyone out there is beating the market,” Lisa remarked. “So why can’t we?”

“Well, for starters,” Scott noted, “when you add up *everyone*, that’s effectively the market, and the market can’t beat itself. So, the idea that everyone is beating the market is a fallacy. The reality is that before costs, the average dollar will earn the market return. After costs, the average investor underperforms as fees, trading, and taxes push results below the market return.”

Lisa’s smile faded. “That sucks.”

Scott elaborated, “While it’s true some investors will outperform, for every winner there must be a loser. It’s just the math of finance.” He paused. “My second question, which market are you measuring yourself against?"

"Uh, the stock market?" Jenn offered hesitantly.

Scott said, "Let me rephrase it. Which specific market or asset classes do you want to compare yourself to? For example, if you owned a fruit basket, you wouldn't compare it to just apples. Same with investing, you need to know what you own, then pick the matching benchmark—apples to apples."

Jenn tilted her head quizzically. "Now I'm lost ... I think I need you to explain."

Scott responded, "Benchmarks are simply reference points for measuring performance. They can track all kinds of asset classes, including stocks, bonds, other financial instruments and even a blend of assets. We often use broad market indices like the TSX 60 or S&P 500, but there are hundreds of benchmarks. So, to figure out if you're beating the market, you first have to know what's actually in your portfolio—and then find or create a benchmark that mirrors your mix."

"For example, when I was in the business, I had clients who would get upset that their portfolio wasn't keeping up with some random benchmark they had chosen. I would explain they didn't *own* that benchmark but held a well-diversified portfolio consisting of Canadian, U.S., and international stocks and funds, bonds, GICs, and cash."

Lisa chuckled. "That kind of sounds like me with my different mutual funds, the money I have in other accounts at the bank and my crypto play account."

"But how do I figure out the right asset mix for me?" Jenn asked.

"There are online questionnaires you can try," Scott suggested, "but your best bet is an in-depth discussion with an experienced industry professional—and someone who is not trying to sell you products."

Scott leaned forward, "My next question is whether you actually want to beat your benchmark?"

Lisa and Jenn answered in unison. "Of course we do!"

"Well," Scott said, smiling, "if you want to beat your benchmarks, you'll need a more hands-on, active investing approach rather than a simpler passive one."

Jenn raised an eyebrow. "Okay, can you explain a bit more about this active and passive investing stuff and how it relates to our benchmarks?"

Passive Investing versus Active Investing

"You don't have to be brilliant, only a little bit wiser than the other guys, on average, for a long, long time."
—Charlie Munger (Warren Buffett's longtime investment partner)

Passive and active investing both have their merits and drawbacks. Choosing between them depends on your goals, risk tolerance, return expectations, and how much time and effort you are willing to commit. There is no right or wrong, and taking a passive or active approach is not necessarily an *all-or-nothing* decision. In fact, many investors find that a hybrid or blending of both styles works best.

Passive: Match the Market, Keep More

Passive investors seek to match the returns of a chosen benchmark instead of trying to outperform it. For example, they may invest in exchange-traded funds (ETFs) that track a specific market index such as the S&P/TSX 60. ETFs offer broad diversification and consistency of returns but limited customization and almost no chance of beating the benchmark. Since many ETFs charge extremely low fees—some less than 0.1% per year—you can consistently earn nearly the full market return at minimal cost and effort. This may not sound thrilling, but studies show that simply matching the market (minus tiny fees) builds a strong, low-stress foundation for long-term success that will produce returns that beat the majority of investors.

Keep in mind that passive investing can be boring and can involve few, if any, changes to a portfolio in a year. For some, this will be a great advantage, but for others, the twin enemies of boredom and *return envy* will cause trouble. For example, hearing about your neighbour or coworker's hot stock tip can tempt you to abandon your plan and chase quick gains, which more often leads to remorse rather than riches.

The bottom line is that a passive approach is low-cost, low-maintenance, and hard to beat. It also comes with fewer regrets if you can resist the urge to tinker.

Active: Try to Beat the Market, Pay More

Active investors aim to outperform the market by actively buying and selling investments based on their analysis and predictions. Active investing offers the potential for higher returns but comes with a much greater risk of underperforming the benchmark. It requires a greater commitment of time and effort, and higher costs for management fees, commissions, and taxes.

All these costs make beating your benchmark that much tougher. The higher the fees you pay, the more the odds favour the market, not you. It is also true that active investing can be very profitable, a thrilling adrenaline rush, a painful financial disaster or all of the above. Proceed with caution and rules.

Know it's not as easy as many think. Bottom line with active investing is that it can deliver big wins but more often delivers higher costs, lower net returns, and sometimes even tears.

The Reality of Beating Your Benchmarks

The only way to beat your benchmark is to be an active investor. In the short to medium term—weeks to a couple of years—there is a high probability that some strategies will beat their benchmarks. Hot market sectors may be experiencing one of their regular bursts of excitement, or your money manager's latest strategy is on fire. Also, over short periods, fees have little effect.

Unfortunately, the cruel teachers of history, and reversion to the mean (which states that asset prices and their returns will eventually return to their long-term average), tend to ruin the party. That hot streak will become cool, your amazing *strategy* will probably blow up, and the odds of continuing to outperform after fees shrink.

Succeeding at active investing requires effort and hard work. You need to know the game you are in because you are competing against well-capitalized, full-time industry pros who spend billions of dollars each year on *market beating* strategies. Despite all this frenetic activity, this group is effectively the market, so before costs, they will earn the average market return. After we count those tens of billions spent on trading activity, fees, market research, and taxes, the average result must be lower. That is a big reason you are likely to underperform your benchmark using high-cost active products.

The investment industry often sneers at retail investors, dubbing them *dumb money*. But a know-nothing investor who knows their limits, and the pros' limits, can beat most of them. At that point, it is no longer dumb money, and when humility beats overconfidence.

One thing the investment industry does well is to measure investment performance. Data shows that the odds of picking a winning manager, after fees, are roughly a coin flip over a medium timeframe of 1 to 3 years. Over longer periods of 10 years or more, less than 20% of active investors outperform in most asset classes.[18] Statistically, it takes 15 years to determine if an investor has skill or is just lucky, but I know few people willing to wait that long.

Scott sat up. "Speaking of data. Did I ever tell you about my MBA thesis back in 1992? It tested the market timing ability of mutual fund managers."

Jenn grinned, "No, but I'm sure you will! Did you learn anything?

Scott replied, "Yes. The main thing was that managers, on average, didn't have any market-timing ability. In studies before then, and since, I haven't seen any credible evidence that overturns that conclusion. Another observation, most of the funds I studied have disappeared through mergers, rebranding, poor performance, or the companies that offered them went out of business."

He added, "When you lack timing ability and then charge high fees, it's almost impossible to beat a benchmark. So, if an advisor says they *beat the market* regularly, that's a red flag. Ask exactly how they do it, ask for their written process, and compare their long-term, net-of-all-fees results to the right benchmark. If they can't show a clear, repeatable process with verifiable results, consider moving on."

Jenn raised an eyebrow. "So, if most don't beat the market, why do we pay them so much?"

Scott chuckled, "Because marketing works better than math!"

Lisa giggled, "Okay, I saw this guy on YouTube sitting in a Lamborghini who said he makes 30% a year."

Jenn smirked at her sister. "If you were making 30% per year like Lambo Bro', why would you bother doing YouTube videos?"

Scott remarked, "Great point, Jenn. Claims don't pay you—results do. What matters is your net, after all costs, versus the right benchmark. Compare your net, not their hype."

How Are My Investments Performing?

To answer your question of *How am I doing?*, do the following steps. For each of your Asset Classes, list the Return and Portfolio Weightings as per the example below. Second, for each asset class, multiply your Return by its Portfolio Weighting to get the Return Contribution for that class. Third, sum up all the contributions to get your Total Gross Return, which is 7.7% in this example. Lastly, subtract any fees and costs to arrive at your Net Return.

Asset Class	Return	Portfolio Weighting	Return Contribution	
Short-term or Cash:	4 %	10 %	0.4 %	(4 % X 0.1)
Fixed income (Bonds/GICs)	5 %	40 %	2.0 %	(5 % X 0.4)
Canadian equities:	10 %	20 %	2.0 %	(10 % X 0.2)
U.S. equities:	9 %	20 %	1.8 %	(9 % X 0.18)
International equities:	15 %	10 %	1.5 %	(15 % X 0.1)

Total Gross Return (0.4% + 2% + 2% + 1.8% + 1.5% = 7.7%)	7.7 %
Less fees and costs	-2.0 %
Net Return after fees and costs	**5.7 %**

If you repeat the above calculation, using the returns of your chosen benchmarks instead of your actual returns for each asset class, you can then make an apples-to-apples comparison of your progress. Feel free to ask your advisor, financial planner or other investment professional should you require assistance.

Setting Realistic Expectations

An *expected return* is what an investor estimates they will earn based on historical rates of return, or anticipated profits or losses from their investments. Although short to medium-term predictions are mostly futile, over the long term, we can use history as a baseline, but not a guarantee. This is crucial for financial planning purposes and deciding how much you will need to save, as well as visualizing your retirement lifestyle.

Historically, inflation has been in the 2% to 3% range, returns for bonds have been in the 3% to 6% range, and equities in the 6% to 10% range. This has resulted in diversified portfolios returning a nominal (i.e. before fees and inflation) 5% to 7% over time.

However, and not to rain on your parade, there are sound reasons future returns may be lower than recent decades. Excessive government spending resulting in larger deficits and debt loads, higher taxation, elevated current valuations in some markets, slower productivity growth, ageing demographics, and significant proposed capital outlays for the climate transition could all weigh on future returns. (Translation: Plan with conservative assumptions, expect a bit less and save a bit more.)

While nobody can predict the future, a useful anchor is the Projection Assumption Guidelines (PAG) published annually by FP Canada Standards Council™ and the Institute of Financial Planning. They synthesize multiple public sources (including CPP and QPP actuarial reports) and 50 years of historical data to create objective planning baselines. Let us look at an example from their 2025 Projection Assumption Guidelines[19] showing the projected returns for a balanced portfolio.

Asset Class	**Projected Return**	**Portfolio Weight**	**Return Contribution**
Short-term	2.4 %	5 %	0.1 %
Fixed income	3.4 %	45 %	1.5 %
Canadian equities	6.6 %	20 %	1.3 %
U.S equities	6.6 %	20 %	1.3 %
Foreign developed-market equities	6.9 %	10 %	0.7 %
Foreign Emerging-market equities	8.0 %	0 %	0.0 %

Total Gross Return	(0.1 + 1.5 + 1.3 + 1.3 + 0.7 + 0.0 = 4.9)	4.9%
Less fees and costs		-1.3%
Net Return after fees and costs		3.6%

While you can insert any percentages you like into the equation above, it is best to err on the side of being conservative and not use return figures that you hope will magically materialize or that someone promises you.

Always calculate your net return as gross returns are meaningless until you subtract the fees. In the example above, if we change the assumed 1.3% fee to 2.5%, your net return would drop to 2.4% (4.9% - 2.5% = 2.4%). In that scenario, your advisor will be earning more than you and your portfolio will earn 43% less over a 25-year period. Please remember that the only controllable variables are the management fees you pay and your asset mix.

Jenn's eyes were a bit glazed over, "My head is swimming. It looked easy to beat the market with all the information available, but I am now sure that the odds are stacked against me. I'm probably not well suited to pursue much active investing on my own, given all the potential pitfalls. I also see that my current advisor likely doesn't have the skill set, tools or the time to outperform. Maybe a more passive approach with ETFs is my best bet?"

Scott stated, "That's certainly a good place to start. Most investors can increase the odds of long-term success by keeping it simple. The retail investment industry and the banks don't really want you to know this because their whole argument for charging you high fees falls apart. Remember that every extra 1% in fees comes directly out of your return, and it compounds against you over time. Lower fees mean more of your money stays invested, working for you instead of your advisor."

Jenn frowned, "It's like the financial industry uses my fear of not being able to do this myself to keep me stuck in expensive funds. Fortunately, I now know I'll almost never beat my benchmarks using their products. Tonight, I'm going to share our chat with Mike, list our actual asset weightings, and compare them to our benchmarks to see how our investments are really doing." She grinned and looked at Scott. "You may get a phone call."

Scott laughed, "Not a problem. We will sort out your benchmarks, crush down the fees you pay, and let compounding work for you."

Scott paused, "Before we finish up, I would like to offer a caveat and bring to your attention that there are some occasions when active investing can work very well. For example, when Nortel made up 34% of the value of the Canadian stock market at its peak on July 26, 2000, it was worth more than all the financial service and resource stocks in Canada, combined."

Lisa's eyes widened. "Wait, 34% of the entire market?"

Scott added, "Exactly. When Nortel crashed by over 90% in about a year, along with other big tech stocks like JDS Uniphase, they dragged the market down by roughly a third. However, if you didn't own Nortel and JDS, your portfolio probably fared just fine."

"That is crazy," Lisa responded. "So, an active investor who avoided that disaster could have beaten the market?"

"Big time," Scott noted. "That is the kind of rare scenario where active investing can outperform, especially over shorter timeframes. If you have a decent historical perspective, pay attention to numbers and not hunches or crowds, you will start to recognize these kinds of outliers when they show up. It's all part of your wealth literacy, so don't dismiss it outright."

Jenn looked thoughtful. "I still like my earlier idea of putting most of my money in a low-cost passive strategy, but now I'm starting to see the advantages of keeping my fingers in the market for when something feels off or is interesting."

Scott smiled. "Sounds perfect. That's what I call a *Core and Explore* approach! The *Core* is the bulk of your portfolio in low-cost diversified funds or ETFs you rarely touch, and the *Explore* is a small slice for well-researched ideas. Remember, you are not trying to outsmart the market, just ready to act when obvious opportunities show up," he paused, "and be sure to stay in your circle of competence."

Lisa's eyes lit up. "I like that. Can we grab another coffee and check out that *Holy Grail* of investing you were talking about?"

Scott replied, "Of course, and I'll add in another crowd favourite, something I call research confusion."

CHAPTER 6

The Holy Grail Illusion and How Research Misleads Investors

The kitchen now smelled of the freshly baked banana bread Jenn had placed in the oven earlier. "Fuel before finance," Jenn declared, topping up everyone's coffee cups. "I promised brunch if we kept today practical. I'd best hold up my end of the bargain!"

She headed to the fridge and pulled out a platter of eggs, sliced avocado, yogurt and a small mountain of fresh berries.

"Looks great, I don't even know where to start," Scott effused.

Lisa laughed, "Knowing you Scott, I'm sure you'll figure it out!"

As Jenn set the freshly sliced banana bread on the table, a sharp crash sounded in the hallway. Jenn winced and called out, "Mike?"

"All good," Mike said, appearing in the doorway with an embarrased grin. "Just my golf clubs. Gravity one, short game zero." He kissed Jenn on the temple and slid into a chair as she poured him coffee. "Yum, banana bread. Smells amazing."

"Hey Mike, we just started talking about the Holy Grail. Sounds like you could have used one this morning?" Scott chuckled.

"Very funny," Mike replied.

Jenn interjected. "You know, Scott, I've been thinking about creating my own Holy Grail of investing after you mentioned this idea last week. It seems simple enough. I figured I just need to invest in some great funds or stocks—something that does better than average. There are so many options. How hard can it be?"

Scott sighed. "In theory, that does sound reasonable, but the challenge isn't just picking a good fund. It's finding a solution that you can keep for the rest of your life."

"So, what should my Grail be?" Jenn asked.

Scott sat back in his chair. "There are three Grails out there. The first and only one that should matter to you is yours. It is not a product list; it's a process you can stick to that gets you to and through retirement intact: peace of mind, sensible allocation, low all-in costs, a few simple investment rules, and maybe a little legacy if that matters to you."

"Number two is your advisor's Holy Grail. That's about business development."

Mike looked dismayed, "And the third?"

"That would be the investment managers. For them, it's all about short-term performance and gathering assets quickly."

Jenn blinked, "So, my Grail does not match theirs at all."

"Exactly," Scott replied.

Lisa smirked. "So basically, everyone's on their own treasure hunt, and I'm not even holding my own map—I'm just carrying someone else's loot?"

Scott chuckled. "Not if you understand the game and realize everyone's chasing something different. Which brings us to the first big problem you'll face when you try, too many choices."

"Too many choices? I thought that was supposed to be a good thing," Jenn said.

The Paradox of Choice in Investing

The paradox of choice is what happens when abundance turns against us. In everyday life, it's just annoying—like choosing between sixty-seven brands of toothpaste or a dozen streaming services. In investing, it's dangerous because you are making decisions that shape your financial future and overall well-being. With an endless menu of stocks, funds, advisors, and clashing opinions, that abundance leads to confusion, anxiety, indecision, and FOMO (Fear of Missing Out)—not necessarily better decisions.

This flood of information can also lead to *analysis paralysis* where fear of making the wrong move becomes the absence of any action. Hesitation and procrastination delay important actions like rebalancing, seizing opportunities, staying invested or making contributions. Compound those delays, and you create one of the biggest destroyers of your wealth: time out of the market. You freeze, the *endless menu* wins, and your delay behaves like another hidden fee.

This takes me way back to my naval training and fire and flood drills, where a clever *shortcut* began with good intentions but went underwater fast.

A Flood of Options

It was a hot, cloudless afternoon in Colwood, British Columbia, and the mood was relaxed. It was Friday, and our training group had big plans to play a bit of football and then go out for beers, a perfect end to a week of training. The sooner we finished the drill, the sooner we'd hit the field.

Suddenly, the shrill cry of "Fire! Fire! Fire!" tore through the air. This was our cue to drop everything, pull on our fire-protective B-gear, and don Chemox, an old-school self-contained breathing apparatus that looked like a pair of external lungs.

As others wrestled into their B-gear, I figured I would get a jump on the weekend, wow the instructors, and put my freshly minted classroom wisdom to work. I sprinted to the nearest Halon fire extinguisher, popped the release valve open and tossed it down the nearest hatch like a depth charge. Back then, Halon was the *Holy Grail* of firefighting. It was fast, clean and ruthless on flames. The catch? It was also ruthless on the ozone layer, which got it banned by the Montreal Protocol in 1994.

At first, the surly Petty Officers training us looked amused by my ten-second, one-man, *solution*. However, it soon became clear that the crusty old seadogs were not pleased with my intransigence for not following the fire drill playbook. They tried to restart the fire, but because Halon is heavier than air, the gases lingered in the training platform long after the flames were out. There would be no second fire drill that day. Brilliant, we were heading home early.

Like all good sailors, they were adaptable and in no hurry to start their weekend. They simply pivoted to another exercise … and my *Holy Grail* of shortcuts had literally sunk to the bottom.

Lesson One: What looks like a shortcut is often a delay in disguise—usually more costly.

"Flood! Flood! Flood!" echoed across the training field.

Flood drills are another beast, and there are no shortcuts. You get drenched as tons of water begin to pour and spray out of what seems like everywhere. As you scramble in the chaos, you are confronted with an array of wooden mallets, planks and plugs of all sizes—and seconds to pick the right ones for the right holes. Despite our frantic efforts, the water didn't stop flowing and rose relentlessly. Then it suddenly stopped.

A flood exercise ended with a pass or fail. If you had plugged the right holes with the right equipment and the water stopped, you passed. If the water kept getting deeper and deeper until an instructor turned it off, you failed. Either way, you would simply be back the next day. More importantly, nobody really drowned or burned in this training platform as it had safety valves and emergency shutoffs to release the water or douse a fire in seconds.

In the real investment world, there are no *reset* buttons or emergency shutoffs. Bad choices can become very costly, quickly, and with no do-overs.

Mike leaned back in his chair. "So, in your story, the fire goes out, the flood wins, and everyone is late for football? Sounds like my last three DIY projects."

Lisa joked, "You really are the guy who reads the last page of the book first and never follows instructions, aren't you?"

Scott grinned. **Lesson Two: Investing is not a drill, and there are no shutoff valves.**

In the real world of investing, just like the flood drill, the choices come fast, the tools can be confusing, and the water doesn't stop because someone flips a switch. A wrong decision can drown your financial future.

Like Halon, many investment strategies can seem brilliant until they are suddenly obsolete or even harmful to your financial health. The real danger isn't just the number of options, it's also who's offering them to you, and what they get out of it. In the investment game, every player has their own goals, their own incentives … and their own version of the Holy Grail. Let's take a closer look at a few of them.

Financial Advisors: When Their Convenience Replaces Your Customization

Have you ever felt like your advisor's advice could have been handed to anyone? You might be right. If we follow the money, we will soon realize most are compensated based on assets gathered and retained, not on your household's outcomes. That incentive makes scaling their Holy Grail: standardized, one-size-fits-many models and less time per client. Efficient for them; not tailored to you.

Fund Managers: When Performance Becomes a Sales Tool

Have you ever noticed *top fund performers* rarely stay on top? That's because the fund manager's Holy Grail isn't your 20-year outcome. It's about short-term relative outperformance that attracts more assets under management (AUM). Win this year, gather assets next year.

For example, according to Morningstar's research, fewer than one in four active funds in most asset classes beat low-cost indices over ten years, and even fewer keep beating them as time goes on.

The uncomfortable truth is that many managers are incentivized to grow AUM, not your net worth. That doesn't make them villains, but it should reset your expectations to focus on your process first, keep your costs low and maintain disciplined behaviour to align to your goals, not theirs.

Scott leaned forward. "There was a modern legend in fund management. It was Jim Simons and his Medallion Fund. Simons was a cutting-edge code breaker and mathematical genius who helped lead the revolution in computer-driven quantitative trading well ahead of Wall Street."

"He proved you could beat the market, but the amount of work involved was dumbfounding. He assembled a team of hundreds who employed trading algorithms to consistently outperform the market. The Medallion fund[20] averaged gross returns of 66% per year from 1988 to 2018, and despite eye-watering management and performance fees, investors still walked away with an astounding 39% per year."

Jenn's eyes widened. "So … why aren't we all in that?"

Scott smiled. "Because you can't be. Medallion Fund was closed to the public and only open to employees of the fund. For the rest of us, it's like hearing about a magic lottery ticket you'll never be allowed to buy. That's the thing—many of the market-beating legends are behind closed doors or retired by the time we know about them, and the ones you can buy often lose their magic when they scale to the mass market."

Lisa smirked. "So basically, the best shows are always sold out before we even know they exist?"

Scott leaned back. "Pretty much, which brings us to the next trap. Believing that more research will automatically lead to better decisions. The truth? Past a point, extra data just muddies the water."

Stock Research: Confusion at Its Finest

Ever notice that for every *must-buy* stock you hear about, someone else calls it a disaster in the making? There are over sixty thousand publicly traded companies worldwide[21], and every major bank, research firm, and media outlet seems to have its list of *top picks*. Like clockwork, millions of confident, often contradictory, reports flood out each year. One analyst says *buy*, another says *hold*, and other flips to *we changed our mind, sell.*

Where does that leave you, the investor trying to make sense of it all? Overwhelmed and confused by facts, figures and narratives.

Your goals are not about selling products or climbing peer rankings. They are personal, meaning your Holy Grail can't be borrowed, bought off the shelf, or outsourced to someone whose priorities do not match your own. It must be built deliberately, with clarity and intention, and be sustainable. That is where we go next.

Crafting Your Own Holy Grail of Investing

Establishing your own *Holy Grail* means accepting that there is no universal or permanent solution—no miracle fund, no secret formula. Think about this: if you discovered the Holy Grail of Investing, would you advertise it to the world? Its edge would vanish the moment it became widely known. That's one paradox of investing success: the more something works, the more people copy it and the faster it stops working.

Jenn said, "Why?"

"Let me explain," Scott replied. "True story—from a brief stretch when I thought I'd found a real Holy Grail."

Mike laughed. "If it involved your golf game, you definitely lost it."

Lisa raised an eyebrow. "Well, tell us already."

Scott shared, "It was when I was a youngish broker at the turn of the century. The Big Five banks—plus the insurance companies Manulife, Canada Life, and Sun Life—started issuing a new kind of junior subordinated debt known as Capital Trust Securities, basically bond-like. They had catchy nicknames like BaTS, BOaTS, CaTS, CLiCS, CoaTS, MaCS, SLEECS, and TruCS."

"At first, they traded on brokerage bond desks and then in 2002, they also started trading on the Toronto Stock Exchange. I don't remember exactly how I came across it, but I noticed the same security sometimes priced differently in the two markets. That created an arbitrage."

Jenn sat up. "What's an arbitrage?

"Great question," Scott remarked. "Arbitrage is exploiting a price difference in two or more markets at the same time. An investor buys where it's cheap and sells where it's dear—it's close to risk-free if done properly."

"Some days my assistant and I made nothing, other days a few hundred, but on many days, we made thousands with just a few minutes of work," Scott said, smiling. "I thought I'd found a Holy Grail. I did the math and got ahead of myself, thinking I'd retire in three years if we could keep this up."

Lisa smiled, "Sounds like you were counting your chickens before they hatched. What went wrong?"

"Competition and rules," Scott replied. "One day, another trader showed up, a month later, another. The cat was out of the bag, and the fat spreads on the buys and sells disappeared. Then the regulators moved all the trading to the stock exchange only. The bottom had promptly fallen out of my Holy Grail."

Mike chuckled, "That sucked. Sounds like the only acronym missing from your junior bonds was RaTS."

Scott laughed, "Exactly. The edge was exhilarating but unfortunately temporary. That's the problem with calling anything a Holy Grail: the moment it's obvious, it's over. Which is why you build your own Holy Grail around consistency, discipline, time-tested principles, clarity and realism. Anchor it with wealth literacy to include an appreciation of market history, the basic theory of how markets work, an awareness of your own psychological biases, and always follow the money."

"Okay, makes sense." Jenn smiled at Mike, "I've decided we're going to create our own Holy Grail!"

Mike grinned and leaned back in his chair, "Alright, dear, I'm curious. What is your version of the Grail?"

Jenn took a deep breath. "For us, the Holy Grail of investing is a solid, long-term game plan built on simple principles and clear rules. An asset mix we can sleep with at night, reasonable expectations, and minimized costs. We'll own a diversified portfolio that we understand—nothing fancy we can't explain. We'll watch out for active investing traps, avoid doing silly things like performance chasing, and be willing to ask for advice when we need it. Lastly, we'll keep improving our wealth literacy, so we can make smarter choices over time."

Mike nodded, "I like it. Let's write it down."

Lisa agreed, "Sis, that's awesome!"

Scott praised Jenn. "I'm impressed! Stick with that focus, and you two will do well over the long run. A portfolio like that will beat a large share of investors with similar goals—not because it's complex, but because it's disciplined, consistent and low-cost."

Jenn's face lit up. "Hey, guys, I'm pumped. I know the morning is pretty much over, but I'd like to keep going today."

Scott acknowledged. "Yeah, I can do that. Let's take a dive into the sales machine and see what tactics they use to get you to pay more."

CHAPTER 7

The Sales Machine Unmasked: How the Industry Tricks You

"I think I prefer tricks over tactics!" Jenn joked.

Scott laughed, "Alright, tricks it is. Let's talk about the machinery behind the message and the tricks that keep you confused, compliant, and just comfortable enough not to push back."

Scott paused for a moment, then added with a half-smile. "It's like J.D. Salinger said in *The Catcher in the Rye* — "All you have to do is say something nobody understands, and they'll do practically anything you want them to."

He looked around the table. "That's the playbook in finance. When clarity dies, sales win."

The Sales Machine in Plain English

The financial services industry profits by confusion. With complicated jargon, cherry-picked data, and buried fees, banks and investment firms make money feel harder to understand than it is. Solid financial advice should be straightforward, but simplicity isn't as profitable, nor does it keep you dependent on their services. Complexity, on the other hand, breeds misconceptions, fear, and blind trust—which the industry exploits to charge unnecessarily high fees, push products you don't need, and rake in billions of excess profits at your expense.

Here are five common tactics used to trick you, not serve you.

Complex Jargon or Confuse First, Charge Later: The industry loves sophisticated-sounding terms and pseudo-technical language because it creates the illusion of expertise. The goal isn't clarity, but dependence. When you are confused, you're less likely to question advice, products, or fees. Always ask questions until you understand. If the explanation doesn't get simpler, it's not for your benefit. Ask your provider, "Please explain this in plain English in two sentences. If it can't get simpler, it's not for me."

The Illusion of Free: If a financial plan is *free* chances are, you are the product. Banks, insurance companies and other financial firms use free planning as a sales funnel to push high-fee mutual funds, insurance policies, or proprietary platforms. That employee may be a commissioned salesperson with a sales quota, not a fiduciary acting in your best interest. Costs can get buried in fund expenses, spreads, trading commissions, or layered advice fees. If it sounds too good to be true, it usually is. For example, some banks now advertise commission-free ETFs, but you still pay M.E.R.s, bid-ask spreads, and any account/platform fees for as long as you own them. You ask, "List, in dollars, every way you and your firm get paid over the next year if I follow this plan."

Another tactic, over the past few years, is numerous companies have emerged offering to help you find a *vetted* advisor at no cost to you. If we follow the money, we'll see advisors and their teams with important-sounding titles, who are charged by these companies for conference fees, coaching, promotional packages, and four-digit subscription fees. For example, some charge licensing fees to advisors (e.g., US$5,500 upfront + US$1,700 annually), after which advisors must buy reprint bundles (e.g., US$2,500 for 100 copies) to distribute the glowing advisor write-ups these companies produce.

The Past Performance Fallacy: Firms routinely cherry-pick time periods to make fund performance look better than it really is. Interestingly, industry and non-industry studies come up with the same conclusion: that the returns of these funds are below average in subsequent time periods and the disclaimer *Past Performance Is No Guarantee of Future Results* rings ever louder. Another quiet strategy is to make underperforming funds disappear. This is accomplished by merging them into better performing funds, rebranding, or a good old-fashioned burial in the *Mutual Fund Graveyard*, so investors only see the survivors—not the failures. Always ask: "What's been excluded from the performance graphs?"

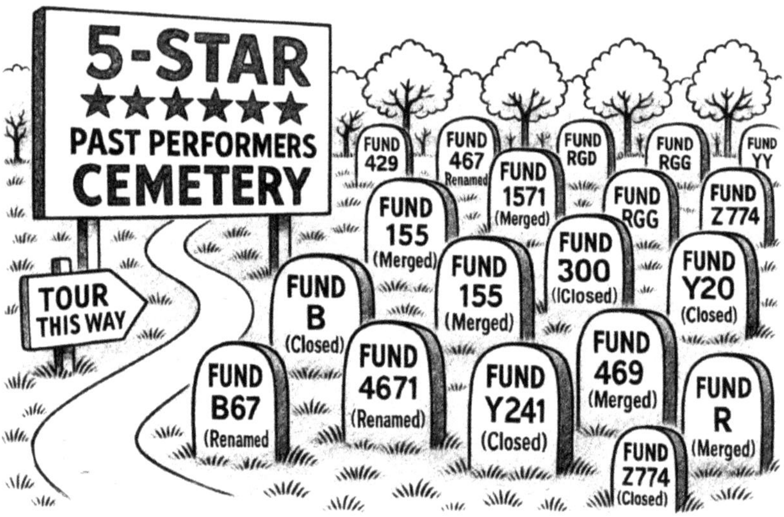

Hiding Fees and Costs: Fees are the silent killer of long-term returns, and they're often buried in the fine print. Whether it's management fees, fund expense ratios, or trading commissions, many firms make all-in costs intentionally hard to find. Websites may list services, but rarely the price. You ask, "Give me a complete, after-fee and after-tax dollar breakdown per $100,000 against a low-cost ETF reference portfolio."

Misleading Advertising and Urgency Tactics: Unsolicited offers, limited-time deals, and emotional promises are all sales tactics disguised as advice. Whether it's a *green* investment that's packed with gas and oil stocks or a *socially responsible* fund that's 90%

branding, much of what's sold to you is more sizzle than substance. The pressure to act quickly is often a red flag. Take your time because real financial decisions don't expire at midnight. You ask, "What specifically changes if I wait for 30 days? What risks increase? And what costs rise?"

More Tricks You Should Know (or *Free* Bonus Round)

Beyond the five main tactics, the industry's playbook has a few more pages:

- High-pressure sales pitches disguised as *just having a chat* or *friendly advice.*
- Affinity pitches that lean on shared communities, backgrounds or identities to build false trust.
- Omission of risks or other key information, and showing only the upside of complex products.
- Bait-and-switch, where you're promised one service but sold something far more expensive.
- Acquisition bias, when new clients or prospects get teaser rates, perks, or faster access, while existing clients get inertia.
- Product bundling *nudges* you to keep your chequing accounts, credit cards, mortgages, investments, and insurance under one roof. Industry studies have shown that once you use four or more products and services with the same financial institution, you are unlikely to switch providers because of the costs, time and forms involved to move your business elsewhere. That *relationship pricing,* so attractive at the start, often becomes a pair of handcuffs rather than long-term savings.
- *Scarcity theatre* is used to inflate perceived demand with tactics such as delayed appointments, wait-lists, or limited openings, e.g. "Only six spots left."

Jenn set down her pen. "Here's my take: if I feel rushed, confused, or dazzled, I'm being sold and not advised. If I can't understand something in two sentences, I pass. Same with anything labelled *free*.

Mike leaned back. "And no more *limited windows*. If waiting 30 days changes nothing real, I wait."

Scott smiled. "Good. Clarity first, then product. If a claim needs jargon, urgency, or theatre to work, it likely doesn't. I'd also add, never sign anything if you don't fully understand it. There is nothing wrong with a *cooling off* period, and they'll wait to get your business if it's legitimate."

Lisa nodded. "I'll be sure to price each product and service individually on one page, after fees and taxes, and in dollars. No more falling for the bundled perks that act more like handcuffs if I try to leave."

Scott stood to stretch and said, "You guys have got it. Next time, let's take a closer look at the second wolf— financial advisors—and see who actually earns their fee."

Suddenly, Jenn's phone buzzed. She picked it up and read the message aloud, "Hi Jenn, it's Suzanne from Jim's office … Jim would like to take you to lunch next week."

Jenn stared at the screen. "Guys … something's up with Jim."

CHAPTER 8

The Good, the Bad, and the Shady: Choosing an Advisor Who Earns Their Fee

At 9:05 a.m. the following Monday, Jenn picked up her phone. "Hello?"

"Hi Jenn, it's Suzanne from Jim's office. Did you get my message?"

"Yes, thanks. Everything okay?"

"Yes, all is good. Jim was hoping to take you out for lunch and give you a quick update. Would the 10th or 11th work?"

"Sure, either day is fine," Jenn replied.

Later that week, Jenn stepped into the Little Italy trattoria and immediately spotted Jim waving enthusiastically. A young woman sat beside him, smiling politely.

"Jenn, over here!" Jim called.

"Hi Jim," Jenn replied. "Thanks for the lunch invite. What's up?"

"Well," Jim blurted, "it's been a great couple of years. This recent market surge has been kind and increased my assets under management significantly, so my payout has gone up huge, and I can retire earlier than I thought. Two months from now, in fact. Sarah here will be taking over your accounts."

Jenn gulped. "Oh, wow … congratulations, Jim ... I guess. What does this mean for me?"

"You'll be fine. Just keep working and adding new money to your accounts. Anyway, Sarah will be great, my manager hand-picked her just for you," Jim reassured.

Sarah extended her hand warmly with a practiced smile. "Jim's told me all about you. I'm looking forward to working together."

Jenn nodded, but her thoughts were already spiralling. She smiled politely through the rest of the meal, her appetite replaced by unease.

Walking back to her car, Jenn quickly texted Mike and Scott in their group chat.

"Guys, I know we were supposed to meet later this month, but we need to talk ASAP. I just lost my financial planner. PLEASE HELP!"

That Sunday morning, after an early round of golf, Scott, Mike and his brother, Phillip, headed back to Mike's place for brunch.

Jenn greeted them at the front walk. "Good morning, gentlemen. I'm surprised to see you, Phillip, but I'm glad you could join us. Is Pamela coming?"

Phillip frowned at his brother, "No, not today. Mike insisted I come over for brunch, he thought I might learn something even though I told him I'm a do-it-yourself investor."

As they walked into the kitchen, the men caught the scent of freshly baked cinnamon rolls. Lisa was seated at the kitchen table, enjoying one of them.

Phillip grinned, "Good morning, Lisa, I hope you left us some!"

Lisa looked up and chuckled, "Maybe one. Great to see you too."

Jenn set her coffee down, suddenly serious. "Well, just when I thought Mike and I were getting on track, Jim dropped another bomb, said he's retiring."

"Did the bank assign you to another financial planner yet?" Scott asked.

"Yeah, but I'm not sure. She's awfully young, and I'm unsure about the fit for our retirement planning." Jenn paused, "We're feeling kind of lost. Mike and have been talking about doing it ourselves, and know we could save thousands per year, but I just don't know if we are ready."

Scott nodded, "Well, that is one option, to do it all on your own. Personally, though, I agree with you that you're not quite ready yet. However, given your recent push on wealth literacy, I do see you doing most of it on your own soon."

Scott paused. "A lot of people take the plunge and do it on their own, but they don't know what they don't know. They don't realize what is being done for them in their current setup. Then a big, usually bad, moment hits, and all the blind spots show up."

Jenn leaned forward in her chair, brow furrowed. "That's what keeps me up at night."

She paused for a few seconds. "Even though the bank assigned me a new advisor, I've also been looking around online. They all seem very qualified with tons of letters after their names, impressive websites, and polished presentations, but after a while, they all started looking the same. How am I supposed to know who's a good match for me?"

Lisa, still licking icing from her fingers, perked up from across the table. "My guy is really nice!"

"That's exactly what I'm afraid of!" Jenn shook her head with a knowing smile. "Scott, can you help me understand what I should be looking for?"

Scott gave a sympathetic smile. "Start with three questions: What kind of experience and qualifications do they have? Will you work well with them? And do they put your interests first?"

"Let's start by sorting through the types of advisors you're going to encounter, and then we can clarify all those confusing titles and designations. It'll make your search a lot less painful."

Know the Players, Read the Cards

"If you've been playing poker for half an hour and you still don't know who the patsy is, you're the patsy." —Warren Buffett

Ah, the financial services industry—a tapestry of personalities. A world where the diligent and earnest rub shoulders with the suave narcissist, the charming sociopath, and, on occasion, a psychopath. Many advisors exude warmth and charisma, but sometimes that charm masks thin competence or misaligned interests.

Today, the industry is exceptionally well funded and backed by countless coaching and marketing teams who teach advisors and managers how to present the perfect textbook persona. In most cases, advisors devote substantial effort to marketing and business development. They are constantly hunting new clients to expand their assets under management (AUM) and to replenish the ranks of those elusive high-value clients who have slipped away to try their luck with another advisor, or to manage their money on their own.

Most advisors start with good intentions, but the allure of big paycheques and managerial *guidance* can quietly override their original purpose and tilt behaviours towards filling their pockets and doing what's best for the firm and not the client. Some are genuine professionals in planning or investing, while others are simply skilled salespeople, especially when proprietary products are involved. Let's meet the three main advisor types and how to spot them.

The Good

The *Professional*—your Sherlock Holmes of advisors—is the gold standard of advisory services. They typically hold rigorous industry designations, such as the Chartered Financial Analyst (CFA) for investment advisory services or the Certified Financial Planner (CFP) for financial planning services. They continue learning after they've met basic industry requirements, and they meticulously evaluate your finances to ensure their recommendations align with your goals, concerns, and risk tolerance.

They follow a clear process, beginning with a written Investment Policy Statement (IPS) and a plan that accounts for tax, insurance and estate considerations. They put your interests first—and anchor their actions in transparency, showing all fees and costs in dollars, not just percentages.

Good advisors prioritize education over entertainment. They unravel complex financial terms, allowing you to make confident financial decisions. Instead of relying on *canned* solutions, they create customized strategies for your long-term financial health, favouring steady growth over risky quick wins. Acting as your financial compass, they guide you toward security. Though uncommon, finding such an advisor is well worth the effort.

The Bad

The *Company Rep* isn't inherently malicious. They are often well-intentioned but under-skilled, lacking the professional environment, experience, education, or commitment to optimize your situation. Conversations with them may feel aimless or jargon-filled, signalling limited expertise. Their advice often mirrors the latest market trends or firm directives, taking a reactive rather than strategic, forward-thinking approach.

Conversely, they may be competent, but if they work for a firm pushing expensive, one-size-fits-all proprietary investments, they will likely fail to align with your specific needs and instead end up promoting their firm's self-serving business model.

The Shady

The *Promoter* is often a skilled illusionist, presenting a captivating facade of wealth and success while concealing their dubious intentions. They can be the smoothest of talkers, adept at selling high-risk, complex investments that promise suspiciously high returns and opaque costs. These products primarily benefit their own bottom line, with minimal disclosure of risks.

Their unethical practices include hidden fees, misrepresentation of qualifications, little transparency, and paperwork games such as pressure to sign quickly or to sign blank forms. They may also use high-pressure sales, unauthorized trading, or excessive trading (churning). Many of these activities can be traced back to poor supervision when managers lack the time, resources, or attention.

Jenn frowned. "I had no idea it could get that bad. Isn't that just reckless or dishonest behaviour? Is it not illegal?"

Scott shrugged. "Exactly. Most shady advisors don't cross the line into outright criminal territory, but some do."

Phillip, his first cinnamon bun consumed, spoke up, "Like who?"

Scott stated, "The most famous was probably Charles Ponzi[22]. Heard of him?"

Lisa grinned. "Wait—that's a real guy? I thought *Ponzi scheme* was just Wall Street slang."

Scott chuckled. "A real guy. He got nailed for dozens of counts of mail fraud in 1920 and was in and out of prison for years. He promised absurdly high returns, then used money from new investors to pay off old ones, stealing millions in the process. Now we have a fraud named after him."

Mike grinned, "Any more recent ones?"

"Fast-forward a few decades, and it got bigger. Bernie Madoff[23] ran what was likely the biggest Ponzi scheme in history, and his investors lost billions. He faked account statements, trades, returns, pretty much everything. Despite repeated warnings from smart people, he fooled just about everyone. He was sentenced to 150 years when it was all said and done."

Jenn blinked. "How does this even happen?"

"Trust. Reputation. And people not asking questions." Scott leaned back. "Same thing happened here in Canada, Earl Jones[24] took $51 million from elderly clients before he was caught and was sentenced to 11 years in jail. The authorities let him out after serving just four years. More recently, Sam Bankman-Fried,[25] a supposed crypto genius. Turns out he was using client funds at FTX like a personal piggy bank. Around $8 billion disappeared, and he was sentenced in 2024 to twenty-five years in prison."

Phillip chuckled and crossed his arms, "I'm guessing there are more stories?"

Scott gave a slow, quiet nod. "Unfortunately, too many to count, but if you learn to spot the red flags, you're already way ahead of most people."

Red Flags: Protecting Your Interests

"The study of money, above all other fields in economics, is one in which complexity is used to disguise truth or evade truth, not to reveal it." — John Kenneth Galbraith

The saying *It sounds too good to be true* exists for a reason. Financial fraudsters have destroyed their victims' lives, often with no recourse, for as long as we have used money. Despite this and the fact that fraud can be complex, it almost always comes with warning signs if you know where to look.

Payee Test: Never pay an individual requesting payments in their name or to an unrelated third party. Payments should go to a verified firm or custodian.

The *Too Nice* Test: Charm is not a credential, and scammers rely on it to disarm skepticism and gain trust.

Office Test: Locations that are vague, sketchy or constantly under renovation are warning signals. Verify.

Transparency Test: Honest advisors disclose all compensation clearly, in dollars. Dishonest advisors will be evasive. If someone says, *No cost to you* beware, as nothing in finance, or anywhere else, is free.

Return-Pattern Test: If an investment's returns seem unrealistically high, oddly steady over time, or are billed as risk-free, use extreme caution.

Registration and Custody: If someone sells securities, places trades, takes custody of your funds, or manages your money, you should verify CSA and/or CIRO registration. If someone provides advice-only planning/education and does not sell or manage securities, verify their advisory or planning credentials.

Complexity Rule: Scammers intentionally complicate things to create an illusion of expertise and credibility. If you can't understand how an investment works after a simple explanation, that's a potential problem. Here's my own personal rule: If I can't understand the basics in two minutes or less, I pass.

Title Trap: Lastly, one of the fastest ways bad actors hide is behind titles. Before you trust a résumé or a smile, decode the letters behind their name.

An Alphabet Soup

Credentials in finance or insurance can be an alphabet soup of countless designations, certifications, and marketing labels. Not all are created equal. Some require years of rigorous study, while others take little time to achieve and are offered by for-profit *educational* providers more interested in selling courses than truly educating advisors. Common, well-recognized credentials include CFA, CFP, PFP, CIM, or CLU.

Sales titles can be even more misleading. A title like *Vice President* or *Top Advisor* may reflect marketing fluff, seniority or sales production rather than licensing, professional competence, or duty of care. Regulators are tightening standards, but you should still treat titles as a starting point, not proof. If you see one on a card, ask what it means and verify the following questions:

Registration & Category: "Where are you and your firm registered? What activities are you permitted to do?"

Supervision & Custody: "Who supervises you? Where will my assets be custodied?"

Compensation: "What will my all-in fee be in dollars and percentages? Do you have any incentives tied to specific products or production tiers?"

Scope vs. Title: "As a planner/advisor, do you hold a recognized credential and provide a written engagement with scope and limits?"

While regulatory oversight helps, Canada's patchwork of regulators, title-protection rules, and private credentials can still confuse investors. The burden falls on you to translate the letters and the titles—or work with a competent advice-only professional planner or advisor who can interpret the alphabet soup for you.

Advisors are Human Too

Making honest mistakes doesn't render someone untrustworthy. Investing is challenging, and even successful fund managers don't always pick winners. Roughly 30 to 40% of positions in any portfolio may lose money or lag the benchmark at any point in time. What matters is that gains on the winners more than offset the losses on the losers. This is why we hold diversified portfolios and judge advisors by process and risk control, not perfection.

Another criterion is how they respond to challenges. A good advisor takes responsibility, explains the lesson, and adapts strategies. A red-flag advisor makes excuses, shifts blame, cherry-picks benchmarks or refuses to acknowledge errors. If they consistently deflect accountability, it's time to walk away.

When mistakes do happen, here are a couple of quick questions to ask your advisor.

1. What did we learn?
2. What will we do differently next time, and when?

Please find a detailed Advisor Selection Checklist on the Resource Hub, Chapter 8, at www.scottross.ca.

Jenn exhaled slowly. "Okay, so process over personality. That helps."

Scott tilted his head. "Bottom line: judge value by evidence, not promises. Fees in dollars, a written process, an understanding of an advisor's qualifications, and ensure their incentives align with your goals."

Lisa raised an eyebrow, thinking it through. "Makes sense. Pay for advice, not sales, and always follow the money. That explains a lot."

Scott responded, "Bingo!"

A beat of silence. Mike raised an eyebrow. "So, what's for breakfast?"

Scott exclaimed, "Conflicts of interest. Bittersweet, full of hidden incentives, and no nutritional label in sight."

CHAPTER 9

Confessions and Conflicts of Interest: More Hidden Drains on Your Wealth

Mike grabbed the fruit salad out of the fridge as Jenn pulled a tray with two quiche pies out of the oven.

Phillip flashed a wide smile. "Those look way better than Scott's idea!" Everybody laughed and dug in.

Jenn asked, "I'm still a bit unclear why we need to know about conflicts of interest. Isn't my bank supposed to have my best interests in mind?"

Scott responded, "They should, but that may not always be the case. Let me explain. A conflict of interest is when someone's personal or professional incentives don't line up with your best interests—whether they admit it or not. In finance, it's not rare; it's baked in."

Mike leaned in. "But aren't conflicts of interest just … part of life?"

Scott nodded. "For sure. They're everywhere. When priorities compete, a conflict can sneak in, especially when money is involved. You need to understand that the financial world isn't designed around your goals. It's built around their goals."

Lisa set her fork down. "So where do those hidden conflicts usually show up?"

Scott replied, "We'll get to that, but first, a few insider confessions to set the stage."

What Your Advisor Would Never Say Out Loud

Much like the figure behind the *Wizard of Oz* curtain, here are a few confessions advisors or planners would rarely admit in public.

"Transparency isn't always my priority. I might suggest an investment opportunity, highlighting potential returns, but gloss over embedded fees, hidden commissions, or penalties for early withdrawals. I know you likely won't read the details buried deep in the fine print of legal documents."

"I've recommended investments *you* later regretted. For example, I enthusiastically recommended investing in tech stocks during the 2000 market surge, convinced they were a *sure thing*. I didn't warn clients like you to reduce exposure, so many suffered significant losses when the tech bubble eventually burst."

"I get paid more to sell certain products, so I do. This directly addresses the root cause of my biased recommendations to you. When a product pays higher commissions, it tempts me to suggest it even though a cheaper or better alternative exists for you. Also, my firm primarily measures success by the gross revenue I generate, so I'm always under pressure to produce fees and commissions."

"I love selling pre-packaged or *canned* investment solutions. My firm often expects me to prioritize our proprietary or pre-packaged investment products even if they are not the best fit for you. The systemic pressure is real."

"Referral fees and kickbacks? I may receive referral fees for recommending certain services. Sometimes, with referrals to other professionals like lawyers or accountants, the kickbacks are not monetary but client referrals in return, a bit of quid pro quo."

"I churn your account to generate more commissions. Excessive trading can create commissions. It usually lessens your outcomes, and it's easy to label it as *active management*. You probably won't know the difference. Let's be honest, it's often more about my income than your returns."

"I focus on my biggest clients first. Smaller clients that don't generate big fees get less time and attention."

Jenn tilted her head. "Are those *confessions* … really true?"

Phillip chuckled. "Well, from my short time working as a junior economist back in the 90's at Dewey, Screwum, and Howe, I'd say they are pretty darn close." Everyone laughed.

Scott smiled and nodded. "Next up, conflicts of interest. They come in all shapes and sizes, and while some are obvious, many are buried under layers of titles, jargon, and firm policies."

Lisa raised an eyebrow. "So, it's not just about shady products or bad advice?"

"Exactly," Scott responded. "There are quieter forces, like sales targets, payouts, and processes that can steer priorities away from yours. Let me show you a few real-world examples."

The Multiple Faces of Conflicts of Interest

How Your Investment Advisor is Paid. If your advisor charges a percentage of assets under management (AUM) their pay rises as your account balance increases. That can tilt recommendations towards keeping your money invested instead of recommending other strategies that might serve you better, such as paying down debt or funding another goal. In some cases, it can even favour a recommendation to leverage your account (i.e. borrow money to invest). Your advisor then collects higher fees given your larger account size, and as a bonus, might get a *gold star* or cross-sell credit for a related loan referral to a local banker they work with. Meanwhile, you now pay more in fees on the larger account, pay interest charges on the money you borrowed, and have been saddled with a higher risk portfolio due to the added leverage.

The industry adores AUM fees for their predictability and has turned them into a modern-day gravy train. Advisors will also focus on increasing your assets, especially when planning to sell their practice to another advisor, as the larger their *book of business*, the more they will be paid when it is sold. Clients should assess whether their advisor's AUM model aligns with their financial goals and consider other compensation structures, such as hourly or flat fees, to find the best fit.

Note: Transaction-based pricing isn't always bad, especially today, given the availability of discount or online brokerages. In past years, paying high commissions for trading often created problems, but today, paying that *one and done* commission might be your best alternative and is much cheaper in the long run than paying ongoing AUM fees. For example, you could pay a commission once to buy an ETF that will be part of your portfolio's core rather than being charged an annual fee for the lifetime of that investment.

Conflicts between Investment Advisors. While advisors may work for the same company, they are not on the same *team*, so to speak. Advisors compete intensely among themselves for clients, and this can sometimes lead to prioritizing their own standing or career growth over clients' best interests. It can also lead to aggressive marketing tactics or negative portrayals of *rival* advisors. For example, there are many instances of advisors obtaining the names of other advisors' clients in their own firm and prospecting them, often fueled by an *every advisor for themselves* mentality. When a colleague falls ill or departs, advisors may rush to claim abandoned client accounts, pitching themselves aggressively—like a game of musical chairs, but with your finances.

Similarly, offers of a *free second opinion* are probably the most common, yet poorly camouflaged, sales tactic designed to transfer your funds to their management. Given the advantage of hindsight, advisors are adept at telling prospective clients what their current advisor did wrong and how they would have done things better for you. Hindsight can be a wonderful prospecting tool.

Conflicts Between the Advisor and the Firm. Many advisors work in environments where they may be pressed to sell proprietary products, cross-sell, or meet internal sales targets. This limits their freedom to offer you the best solutions, and you may never see the full menu.

Conflicts Arising from Personal Relationships and Interests. When an advisor or their firm has a personal tie to a product or provider, recommendations may tilt, even unintentionally. These ties may include:

- An equity stake or revenue share from a fund or product provider.
- Relatives or friends employed by a provider or referral partner.
- Outside business activities, such as serving on a board or running a side venture like distributing insurance/mortgages through an affiliated entity.
- Selling *in-house* solutions when comparable, lower-cost options exist.
- Inviting clients into private placements which the advisor also participates in or profits from.

Ask for a written related-party disclosure listing any ownership, referral compensation, or outside roles (including household members), and how your data is kept confidential. Require that any conflicted recommendation be accompanied by a comparable, unconflicted alternative with full fees and risks disclosed.

Conflicts Arising from Third-Party Relationships and Third-Party Referrals. There is nothing wrong with making a referral if it genuinely serves the client's interests when they need another product or service. Conflicts arise when that referral comes with compensation, whether it be from fees, revenue-sharing, or reciprocal favours. This conflict further deepens if there are better alternatives available.

A newer and increasingly popular wrinkle is the *no-cost* advisor-match website. Behind the promise, your details are often routed through a pay-to-play lead auction and provided to the highest-bidding advisor—not necessarily the best fit for your situation. These *free* services are frequently sponsored and are rarely designed to be objective.

Conflicts from Mixed and Multiple Service Offerings. When advisors offer a mix of services (investment advice, lending, tax planning, insurance, estate planning), they may push the products or services that generate the highest fees or commissions and create the least amount of work. That can mean more time spent on things that pay (new policies, fund switches, loans) and less on things that don't (tax-loss harvesting, beneficiary reviews, estate document follow-through, etc.), which can leave gaps in your overall financial plan.

What can you do? Ask for a written service matrix (what's included/excluded and how each item is compensated). Separate advice-only planning from product sales, request itemized hours for planning tasks, and require a comparable, unconflicted alternative with full fees and risks listed for any product recommendation.

Educators and Regulators: Structural Incentives to Watch. Even educational institutions and regulatory bodies can face conflicts of interest. Organizations claiming to be independent or unbiased may be owned or controlled by entities with financial incentives, thus influencing their teachings or policies. For example, the Canadian Securities Institute (CSI), one of the most established and long-time educators of financial industry employees in Canada, was purchased in 2010 by Moody's Corporation,[26] a U.S. publicly traded company. Subsequently, in August, 2025, CSI was again sold to another American company, Fitch Learning.[27]

"That was eye-opening," Jenn said. "I had no idea so many hidden incentives and conflicts were at play."

"So," she continued, "if I've got this right, we need to watch not just what an advisor tells us, but also for what they aren't saying because of all these behind-the-scenes pressures."

"That's right," Scott chimed in. "Do not feel intimidated. Ask how they are paid, what quotas or targets they face, and what alternatives they considered. Always follow the money."

Mike nodded. "So, we should ask how independent our advisor really is, whether they must meet sales quotas, if they earn referral fees, and any other conflicts they might have, right?"

"Yes! If they say they have no conflicts, that's your first red flag," Scott noted.

"Makes sense," Lisa agreed. "Maybe next time, I'll work with someone who is compensated like me. As an accountant, I only get paid for the work I do. I certainly don't get paid based on how much my client happens to be worth."

Phillip smirked, "All of the above are why I do it on my own."

Mike frowned at his brother. "And you know everything as well?" Phillip winced.

"Easy on Phillip," Scott chuckled. "Anyway, there's one more area I want to cover before any of you start an advisor search. You're going to come across truly incredible marketing with slick websites and shiny brochures. It can get really confusing."

Jenn turned to Lisa and Phillip. "You two good to stick around for this part?"

Lisa replied, "For sure, sis."

Phillip tilted his head, "This should be good. Fire away, Scott!"

CHAPTER 10

Lies, Damned Lies and Investment Advisor Marketing

Scott stated, "I've reviewed a lot of advisor and planner websites over the years and on more than a few, I am quite sure the sales pitch mirrors the planner's own dreams, not yours."

"As in," Jenn exclaimed, "Welcome to my fantasy that you're paying for!"

Scott laughed. "Exactly. It reminds me of a well-known 1940 financial industry classic, *Where are the Customers' Yachts?*[28] In many ways, not much has changed. Advisors are still thriving on separating you from your money."

"That," quipped Phillip, "is darkly amusing."

"It is?" Scott smirked. "Let's get right into the specifics."

Lies, Damned Lies, and Cherry-Picked Truths

"There are three kinds of lies: lies, damned lies, and statistics."
—Benjamin Disraeli, British Prime Minister 1874-1880

The above quote was further popularized by Mark Twain and is intended to highlight the persuasive and slippery power of statistics to decorate weak arguments. Just as an expert in numbers can twist statistics to paint almost any picture, many advisors and planners will spin a tale you want to hear: A bright financial future framed by exaggerated claims of superior performance and service.

This chapter is a wake-up call to help you navigate the murky waters of investment advisor marketing with skepticism and critical thinking. Each year, most advisors will spend tens or even hundreds of thousands of dollars to promote themselves and increase assets under management. This leaves unwary consumers confronting a marketing landscape that is rife with distortions and half-truths.

Deceptive Promises: Exposing Empty Claims

Some advisors make bold and confident predictions about future market movements or promote proprietary investment strategies rooted in expertise. It's one of the easiest myths to sell, and one of the most damaging to buy. In reality, no one can reliably forecast all cycles, crises, or market turning points.

For example, I once came across an advisor's website stating: "Our macro-economic perspective provides the foundation for forecasting and navigating all types of economic cycles and crises."

While it might sound convincing at first, that kind of capability doesn't exist, and markets have a way of humbling everyone. Hire someone who has a disciplined process, not someone who claims they have a crystal ball.

Other promises inflate credibility by padding credentials or using impressive-sounding titles, such as *Top Advisor*, that reflect sales performance more than professional mastery. Some also target specific market segments, falsely claiming expertise or specialization. A common line is "We are leading specialists for small business owners, entrepreneurs, and high-net-worth families." While this may sound inspiring, these claims require little or no proof of actual ability or expertise and are made eagerly because these segments are lucrative and easy to market to.

Optimistic predictions and catchy titles will get an initial prospecting meeting for an advisor, but time and workload will eventually determine your investment results. Let's pull back the curtain and see how advisor hours are really allocated, and what that means for your success.

Behind the Curtain: Where the Hours Go

Advisors are human with finite hours. That can create a gap between promises and the delivery of services to you. To help, many advisors operate with large teams, sometimes with a dozen or more employees, allowing them to leverage their time and serve more clients. This may also lead many clients to incorrectly assume they are paying *top dollar* for access to the expert. The reality is that individualized attention from the lead advisor is often severely limited, as many advisors serve 200 to 300 clients.

When you add time for client meetings, staff management, administration, compliance, and account oversight, there are often not many hours left for the advisor. Many successful advisors limit their client-facing hours significantly for lifestyle commitments and other non-client activities, such as abundant vacation time, golf, fishing trips, triathlon training, or travel, often to and from their second homes. In addition, many spend a large share of their week on *business development* (a.k.a. schmoozing and prospecting) because that is what grows a book of business and advisor income most quickly. Your takeaway: an advisor can be very *successful* by industry revenue metrics without that success equating to your results or the value you receive.

Many advisors lean on another well-worn tactic: controlling the narrative through what they choose to share—and more importantly, what they don't.

Selective Disclosure: Hiding the Truth

Another common tactic advisors use is selective disclosure, such as highlighting favourable details while conveniently omitting critical information. This *trick of the trade* distorts a client's understanding of risk and return and undermines trust in the advice itself.

A favourite strategy of advisors is to create the illusion of investment prowess by cherry-picking convenient start and end dates, thereby making reported returns appear both higher and smoother than they are. Performance is a mug's game, and Murphy's Law all but guarantees the advisor's returns will decline right around the time you hand over your account

Another tactic is to borrow others' successful strategies and present them as their own. For example, I knew an advisor who would routinely show prospects the impressive performance of a single client account while omitting the fact that the strategy had been developed entirely by the client, and not the advisor.

Like all CFA Charterholders, I had strict guidelines about what performance metrics I could share with any prospect or client. Meanwhile, advisors operating under looser standards can showcase questionable investment track records, leaving you to guess what's real and what's marketing spin.

Lastly, selective disclosure frequently applies to fees and costs. Advisors may downplay or obscure the all-in costs, making it nearly impossible to really see how fees quietly erode your returns.

Jenn quipped, "Okay, I officially feel like I've been tricked, somehow."

"I'm still stuck on the fee thing. Like ... how is that even legal?" Lisa hissed.

"It's not always what they hide—it's also what they don't say aloud. That silence is its own tactic," Scott replied.

Mike crossed his arms. "So, basically, if you're not asking the right questions, you're just walking into a financial escape room with no clues."

Lisa grumbled, "And your advisor's the one who built the room."

Scott nodded grimly. "Exactly. And just when you think you've found the exit, they hit you with emotional manipulation."

Phillip retorted, "What kind of manipulation are we talking about?"

Manipulative Techniques: Psychological Games Advisors Play

When partial truths aren't enough to seal the deal, some advisors escalate to psychological levers—from fear-based tactics that prey on anxiety to high-pressure pitches designed to create urgency and bypass your better judgement.

Advisors often rely on emotional language or storytelling to evoke excitement, greed, or fear, all tapping directly into your emotional weak spots. By exploiting these emotions, investors are nudged towards impulsive or irrational decisions that don't align with their long-term financial goals. Typical examples include doom-and-gloom scenarios or overstating the consequences of not following their advice.

Advisors also exploit authority bias by positioning themselves as experts or industry leaders. They cite their credentials, affiliations with prestigious institutions, or years of experience to establish credibility and persuade you to defer to their judgment. This authority positioning is often used to short-circuit critical thinking and elicit unquestioned trust.

Some advisors intentionally obfuscate investment products or strategies with complexity, technical jargon, and mystique. Their goal? Get you to stop asking questions if it seems complicated enough.

Jenn shrugged. “I think I’ll stick with my new advisor, Sarah, for now and give her a chance. This advisor search thing is time-consuming and laced with pitfalls. I might be better off spending my time improving my own knowledge.”

“Fair enough,” Scott responded. “Just make sure you meet with her one-on-one, without Jim. That way, you can really see her process. A casual lunch isn’t a litmus test.”

Lisa looked at her sister, “Be sure to get a one-pager from Sarah that lists her fees versus a low-cost ETF portfolio, describes who does what on her team, how her investment guidance is produced, and how many hours she’ll spend on your file each year, and when.”

Scott smiled at Lisa, “Yes, process beats promise. Every time.”

Phillip sat up, “With all these marketing tricks, manipulation tactics, and backdoor pay-to-play schemes in full swing, isn’t someone regulating all this to protect us?”

“Thanks, Phillip. A great lead in to our next get together when we’ll take a closer look at the third wolf: government, and how they do and don’t protect you and your money.” Scott added, “We’ll also learn how the loving arms of government are shaping your ability to build wealth.”

Everybody chuckled as they rose from the table. Jenn commented, “I’ll send everybody details on the group chat—and Phillip, bring Pamela next time.”

CHAPTER 11

Guardians or Gatekeepers: Who's Really Protecting Your Money?

Lisa knocked once and let herself into her sister's home. "Good morning, Jenn."

"In the kitchen!" came Jenn's voice.

Lisa set her bag down and walked in, smoothing a strand of hair. "Scott not here?"

Jenn shook her head. "Nope. He texted he would be a couple of minutes late."

"Oh ... just wondering." Lisa blushed, watching the kettle's steam, hoping for a distraction.

The doorbell rang, and Jenn smirked. "Saved by the bell this time," as she headed toward the front door.

"Good morning," Jenn greeted Scott. They walked back to the kitchen.

Lisa stood and smiled softly, "Hi, Scott, I'm glad you could make it."

He met her eyes for a beat. "Morning, Lisa, sorry I'm late."

Pamela stepped in right behind him and unbuttoned her coat. "Sorry, traffic was a mess and thank you for inviting me this morning. I'm not sure if Phillip told you, but I just started as the membership coordinator at the City Business Association and figured Scott's sessions would help me better serve our members."

Jenn asserted, "I like your attitude, Pamela. Our husbands, Mike and Phillip, on the other hand, chose golf over government this morning." Everyone laughed.

Scott tapped his folder. "Well, ladies, today's wolf is in Ottawa, our provincial capitals, city halls, basically everywhere. First up, the regulatory framework that claims to protect your money!"

Jenn chimed in, "Government and my money. A classic pairing."

Pamela sat up a little taller, "Sounds good, but I thought regulators and advisors protected us?"

"In theory," Scott replied. "In practice, there are holes you can drive a truck through. Most rules police legality, not value. It's fairly easy for someone to follow the rules and still fleece a client."

Jenn crossed her arms. "So, regulators might not be enough?"

"Exactly," Scott said. "Many are excellent, but they're often outnumbered. Often, they are funded by the very firms they oversee, so it's a bit like the wolves paying the shepherd. Your vigilance is your best defence."

He paused. "At the end of the day, you are the one who cares most about your money." Scott chuckled, "Although, I have seen cases where family members care too, especially those whose favourite investment vehicle is called inheritance."

Lisa commented. "That ... is harsh."

Scott nodded. "Harsh, but sadly, true. Financial elder abuse is more common than most families realize. The good news is that most financial firms are now improving protections, but they can't stop family feuds."

Lisa looked down. "So, what can we all do?"

"You learn. You ask questions. You verify, and you never assume someone else is protecting you, regardless of your age," Scott replied. "Let's map the watchdogs. Who does what and where you stand."

The Watchdog Maze and Finding the Right Door

"I don't want to have anything to do with the government. And yet if we don't have any regulations, there goes civilization, there goes

security, and there goes protecting you against what people are going to sell you."
—Charles Grodin, Actor and Political Commentator

On paper, Canada's financial regulators protect consumers, ensure fair markets, and uphold trust. In practice, the system is often a tangle of federal agencies, provincial commissions, and self-regulators, each guarding a slice. This patchwork approach can open the door to what's known as regulatory arbitrage where firms steer you towards looser rules. Protections can also vary by product, seller, and jurisdiction, so two investors can get very different safeguards for similar risks.

Surveys show many Canadians believe they have no organization to turn to when something goes wrong. This is not true. You simply need to remember that channels do exist, as we will see below.

(Author's Note: Parts of this and the next chapter may seem political. They aren't. The "government wolf" doesn't care about party colours or how you vote—it cares about incentives and your money. Our focus is simple: measurable results for your household. Thank you.)

OBSI (Ombudsman for Banking Services and Investments): Your main external point of escalation.[29] As of November 1, 2024, OBSI is the sole external complaints body for federally regulated banks. For investments, OBSI can recommend compensation (up to $350,000), but recommendations are generally non-binding. If a firm refuses to pay an adequate amount, you may need to negotiate further or pursue legal action. Regulators are currently working toward a binding model for investment cases. This would be a huge win for consumers should it be enacted.

CIRO (Canadian Investment Regulatory Organization): Formed in 2023 through the merger of the Investment Industry Regulatory Organization of Canada (IIROC) and the Mutual Fund Dealers Association of Canada (MFDA). CIRO regulates investment and mutual fund dealers and their registered individuals and serves as the regulation services provider (trading rules and surveillance) for equity marketplaces that retain it. CIRO accepts complaints about rule breaches and can discipline firms/individuals, but compensation for clients typically runs through the firm and/or OBSI.

CDIC (Canada Deposit Insurance Corporation): Insures eligible deposits at member institutions for investors of up to $100,000 per depositor per insurance category per institution. It also covers deposit-taking institution failures but not bad advice or market losses.

CIPF (Canadian Investor Protection Fund): Protects *missing property* up to $1 million per account category if a CIRO-member dealer firm becomes insolvent. This dealer-insolvency coverage does not cover fraud, bad advice, or poor investment outcomes.

FCAC (Financial Consumer Agency of Canada): Promotes financial literacy and enforces federal consumer protection rules in the banking sector. While it provides guidance and oversight on banking consumer rights, it is not where investment representatives are disciplined.

CSA (Canadian Securities Administrators): The CSA is a coordinating body for thirteen provincial and territorial securities regulators, such as the OSC (Ontario Securities Commission). The CSA's mandate is to harmonize securities rules across Canada and to support the smooth operation of capital markets. Your province's securities commission is another option for guidance.

OSFI (Office of the Superintendent of Financial Institutions): Oversees federally regulated banks, insurance companies, and private pension plans. It works with the Bank of Canada and the Department of Finance to ensure the safety of financial institutions. It is not a forum for consumer complaints.

Now that you have met the bodies who can help you, let's take a closer look at the outcomes they produce.

Slaying the Gordian Knot: Regulatory Objectives vs. Investor Outcomes

If you browse Canadian regulators' sites or government ministers' mandate letters, you'll often see visions that emphasize financial system health, and budgets skewed to dealer supervision, enforcement, and market plumbing. By contrast, peers like Luxembourg's Commission de Surveillance du Secteur Financier (CSSF)[30] or Australia's Securities and Investment Commission (ASIC)[31] explicitly target good consumer outcomes and household control. That's the direction Canada should copy.

The federal and provincial governments should modernize mandates so after-fee, after-tax outcomes sit alongside market integrity and system stability, and *encourage* the industry to compete on clarity and value, not complexity. Canada doesn't need more agencies; it needs clear mandates tied to household results. A guiding test: Does this regulation or decision benefit Canadian investors? If yes, proceed.

Before the defenders of Bay Street leap to their ramparts and hoist the *strong banking system* banner, let us be clear. No one is arguing against financial strength and stability, but a fix to mandate that household financial health stand alongside the system's stability. This balance can be corrected, and here is an example of a concrete starting point.

Despite a much lower GDP per capita and a weaker currency, Canadian banks still earn roughly 15% more profit per person in U.S. dollars than their U.S. peers. In plain English, we earn less, our dollar buys less, and yet our banks earn more from each of us. The result is a rock-solid banking system that's more costly than necessary for Canadians. The wolves earn more, and you have less in your pocket.

Three Elephants in the Room: Titles, Fees, and the Illusion of Protection

Scott opened his folder and held up a cartoon of three elephants in neckties standing over a wallet.

Lisa laughed, "Wait, elephants?"

"Yes," Scott grinned. "I'm not exactly sure how it has happened, but for decades three forces have been trampling over the interests of Canadian savers and investors."

"Elephant one is titles. In Canada, almost anyone can offer money advice with a professional-sounding label. There's no consistent national standard like other professions, such as doctors or accountants."

Lisa blinked. "So, the guy managing my RRSP could be using a title that means little?"

Scott shrugged. "Often, yes. There are reforms underway, but it's still a maze for the investing public."

Scott tapped the next elephant. "Now, elephant two is fees and costs."

Lisa frowned. "But I've never gotten an actual bill."

Scott pointed at the table. "Exactly. Unlike other professionals, you rarely get a one-page invoice with an hourly equivalent. If banks showed an hourly equivalent, there'd be riots at the teller line."

Scott tapped the third elephant. "The illusion of protection. Most people assume that financial institutions act in your best interests.

Unless someone is a fiduciary, their bar is *suitable*, not the best or most cost-effective for you. That gives advisors more flexibility but less protection for you."

Pamela noted, "But the regulators could fix that, right?"

Scott nodded slowly. "They could. Plain-language fee disclosures, standardized titles, and a universal best-interest duty would help—but we still don't have one standard across the board."

Pamela sighed. "So, we've got lots of confusing titles, invisible fees, and a system that is not necessarily designed to work in our best interest."

Scott smiled faintly. "That's the herd, now stomping around in your wallet!"

Jenn stirred her coffee. "Why not fix it?"

Scott shrugged. "Because in many cases, regulators are funded by the financial institutions they are supposed to be watching. A bit like the foxes guarding the henhouse with your nest egg inside."

Be Your Own Regulator

Lisa furrowed her brow. "So, if I have a problem, my first step is to talk to my advisor. Second, their manager or the firm's complaint office, and lastly a regulator or dispute-resolution body."

"Yes." Scott leaned back in his chair. "It can often feel like a maze, and OBSI will often be your first stop, but don't worry about picking the wrong door. They will point you in the right direction."

Scott added. "You do have other options, like legal action, but that can be very time-consuming and expensive. Consider it a last resort. Use dispute-resolution first. It's usually funded by the institution you have the issue with, but be aware most cases are limited to recommendations, not enforceable orders."

Jenn leaned in. "So really, the best thing is to be proactive and avoid ever getting into a conflict with your financial provider in the first place? We should do our homework before we ever hire anybody, right?"

"Great point," Scott agreed. "Start by verifying their experience and get their standard of care in writing. Ask what licenses they hold, how they're paid, and whether they're held to a fiduciary standard."

Lisa raised an eyebrow. "And if they get defensive when I ask?"

Scott elaborated, "That's your red flag. A good advisor welcomes smart questions. A slick one will dodge them."

Jenn asked, "And if they are vague about fees or can't clearly explain their services?"

"Run!", Scott responded. "You wouldn't hire a contractor who wouldn't lay out the scope and price. Your money deserves the same clarity."

Jenn raised her mug. "To staying sharp."

Lisa clinked hers in return. "And not getting trampled by elephants. What's next? The growing government section?"

Scott chuckled, "How did you know?"

CHAPTER 12

The Expanding State: Your Shrinking Investment Opportunities

Scott settled in with his second coffee. "Let's keep the morning moving. Here's a quick story from when I was a kid, then straight to what it means for your money."

Jenn grinned, "I'm surprised you can even remember that far back."

Scott chuckled. "I lived in a little southwestern Ontario town, and we had maybe eight TV channels, and half were fuzzy. So, on October 17, 1977, when the Parliamentary channel[32] appeared, it was a big deal."

Pamela looked horrified. "You watched that?"

Scott grinned, "I did. I was a curious kid. I figured Parliament was full of smart people solving important problems. I thought I would learn something." Everyone laughed. "Spoiler alert, I did, just not what I expected. I saw a circus of thumping, heckling, napping, and enough empty chairs to make you wonder if Parliament was secretly held in a ghost town. I was soon debating with myself if Parliament was worse than the school playground at recess."

Lisa grinned. "And?"

"The kids won. Parliament was louder, a lot less fun and put holes in your pockets," Scott joked.

Lisa raised an eyebrow. "So, what's changed?"

Scott sighed. "Probably not much except for higher stakes and bigger bills. I'd also add, less focus on how policies affect Canadians on a day-to-day basis."

Pamela asked, "Why does this even matter?

Scott frowned, "We do need government for certain tasks, but a bloated and expanding government will lower our living standards and make an even bigger dent in your portfolio."

He paused, "Let's take a look at some of these issues, only enough to scratch the surface, but you'll get the idea!"

Pamela replied, "We also know that cutting spending has been nearly impossible lately. It's become a race to out-promise and out-spend."

Scott nodded, "You are right. The third wolf is on an unsustainable path. We now need leaders who will optimize governments' operations, starting with sound policies and not ideologies."

Jenn asked, "So where do we start and how do you tell if a policy is even worth supporting?"

Scott smiled. "Funny you should ask."

The Litmus Test: Is this Good for Canadians?

Imagine if every month, Members of Parliament had one simple job: work across party lines and deliver at least one solution that passed a single litmus test:

"Does this policy improve the long-run prosperity of all Canadians, or diminish it?"

Strong policies clear at least seven tests—growth, incentives, simplicity, predictability, fairness, value and accountability. If a policy bloats costs, adds red tape, or shifts risk to the future, it likely hurts your portfolio via lower growth and higher taxation. Many policies in place today would not make the cut, which helps explain why prosperity has quietly stalled out despite higher taxes and endless promises.

The good news? It's reversible if we stop pretending the status quo works and judge policies by outcomes, not speeches or ribbon cuttings. To course-correct, we need to ask another question that matters: "How does this policy change the conditions where prosperity either thrives or withers?"

Setting the Stage: How Governments Build or Break Prosperity

Governments keep society orderly, but they do not directly create wealth. They are also key to setting the conditions under which citizens and businesses thrive, or don't. This is not controversial—it is basic economics. New wealth comes from the private sector, where people, capital, and ideas produce more with less and create new opportunities.

Think of government as the stage crew in a theatre. When they do their job well, they're invisible: setting the lights, balancing the sound, making sure the whole production runs smoothly so the actors (the nation's citizens and businesses) can shine. Done poorly? They're tripping over cables, killing the spotlight, and handing out tickets to a show no one wants.

Citizens, voters, and investors, should expect and demand fair (not punishing) taxation, clear rules, a stable legal and financial framework, and incentives that reward work, savings and investment. Too often in Canada today, the system is overextended and costly and does the opposite.

The reasons aren't mysterious nor a secret. When government gets too big, too expensive, or fuzzy about its role, capital leaves for where it's treated best—after tax, after regulation, after uncertainty. Investors feel this as fewer quality opportunities and lower after-tax returns.

Another symptom of a poorly run government is how big of a slice of the year you work for the government before yourself.

Six Months with Little to Show

Tax Freedom Day marks the point in the year when the average Canadian family has earned enough to cover its total annual tax bill across the federal, provincial, and municipal levels of government. This includes income and payroll taxes, property taxes, sales taxes to include those on investment management fees, corporate taxes, and the endless drip of consumption taxes on gas, liquor, and everything in between.

In 2025, Tax Freedom Day fell on June 9, six weeks later than in 1961 (May 3). Despite collecting more than five months' worth of the average family's income, governments still ran deficits. If budgets were balanced by taking more days for taxes, Tax Freedom Day would shift 12 days to June 21. For millions of higher-income households, their tax-freedom date effectively drifts into July.

Please let that sink in. Half a century ago, Canadian families paid out approximately four months of their earnings. Today, it's almost 6 months, or about fifty percent more than your grandparents paid. Less money for you, and even less money compounding in your favour.

This trajectory is not sustainable—not for young Canadians just entering the workforce, not for families trying to build a future, not for anyone trying to create a nest egg, and certainly not for any version of *prosperity* our political leaders are still pretending we are headed towards. Follow the money, and the problem isn't only the tax take; it's the expanding scope of public spending and obligations—diffuse, often opaque liabilities that shift costs forward and erode accountability.

Overspending and Underperforming: How Big Government Crowds Out Growth

Back in January 2010, *The Economist*[33] devoted an issue to the dangers of big government, warning: "The rich world has a clear choice—learn from the mistakes of the past, or else watch Leviathan grow into a true monster."

Today, Canada is perilously close to proving that warning right. Governments increasingly focus on keeping voters happy with headlines that are ideologically appealing but often put sustainable economic policies last. It's a costly, modern-day version of ancient Rome's *bread and circuses*. Examples include pandemic-era relief extensions, excessive tariff war subsidies, open-ended EV subsidies, soaring marginal tax rates, and punitive levies on targeted homes.

Lisa squinted. "Didn't we used to be, like, a model economy?"

Scott replied, "Yes, but now we are used as a cautionary tale. Other countries have grown their economies and boosted real per capita incomes over the last decade, but Canada has fallen to the bottom of the barrel.[34] If we adjust for hours worked, we look even worse off."

Scott continued, "People and capital vote with their feet and we have become a country where Canadians and foreigners alike are hesitant to invest. The result has been many talented people leaving, and more money going abroad than coming in."

Pamela sighed. "That is not just a slide but a signal. A stagnant standard of living, rising debt loads, and questions about our fiscal credibility. Sounds like we are setting ourselves up for a crisis."

Scott grimaced, "Yes, it has happened before. The last time was in the mid-1990s. Our dollar was labelled *the peso of the north*. It tanked, interest rates spiked, and our creditworthiness came under fire."

Lisa smirked, "Wait, was our dollar really called that?"

"Oh yeah. Not our proudest moment. Today, we are uncomfortably close to a repeat, but with more bloated spending, way more debt, and fewer options," Scott commented. "Back then, quick policy changes led by Jean Chretien and Paul Martin averted the final act, but many investors paid a price."

Canadian government officials sometimes try to persuade markets and voters that our fiscal situation is stronger than it is. First, is *net debt* accounting. On paper, Canada ranks 5th out of 32 OECD[35] developed nations in fiscal health because calculations often count pensions and the more than $800 billion held in the Canada and Quebec Pension Plans as assets available to offset public debt. The reality, those assets exist to pay your pensions, not the general expenses of Ottawa. If we remove those pension assets from the ledger, Canada falls to 26th out of 32 nations for gross government debt, according to the IMF.

Second is split budgets. Governments increasingly separate operating and capital budgets. Done well, this fosters prudent economic management. Done with political intent, it can obscure structural deficits and relabel reckless spending as *investment*. It will take a bit more accounting creativity to pull the wool over Canadians' eyes.

Government Pensions Are a Taxpayer Liability

More than one Canadian expert has warned that many federal employee pensions are less well-funded than publicly claimed, with hidden liabilities estimated to be in the hundreds of billions of dollars. This shortfall exists even though the substantial majority of all the pension assets in Canada are earmarked for the retirees of various public sector unions, who only comprise a minority of Canadian workers.

An example, in late 2024, the federal government announced that the Public Service Pension Plan (PSPP) had an *excess surplus* of 26.3%[36] or approximately $39 billion. Given that this figure exceeded the 25% surplus threshold allowed by the Income Tax Act, the government transferred the *extra* $2 billion into general revenues to reduce the federal deficit.

That sounds great, but if we use realistic market-consistent valuations, the surplus turns into a $33 billion deficit. The plan wasn't necessarily overfunded; it was underfunded, and taxpayers are potentially on the hook for this massive shortfall. Many government pensions still rely on outdated formulas and assumptions for longevity, inflation, and discount rates, which means that at some point higher taxes or reduced government services may be required to keep these plans solvent.

Here is another example. Many public-sector pensions are based on an employee's best five years of income. Let us imagine you are in the private sector and get a big raise five years before retirement—then a magic agency swoops in and retroactively increases your RRSP limits, as if you had been earning that salary all along. Miraculously, it then adds a massive top-up to your savings.

Sadly, that's not how retirement works—unless you are in a public-sector defined-benefit plan with this feature. There is no Department of RRSP Backdating and Surprise Windfalls for private citizens, but in many government plans, that is what is happening. These top-ups are paid by you. They can add up to hundreds of thousands, and even millions, in lifetime benefits for individual members, depending on their years of service and the size of late-career pay increases. For private-sector taxpayers, the net effect is higher future tax liabilities or reduced services as funding gaps are socialized. This results in less money for your own retirement as you pay more taxes. While this is legal, is it equitable for everyone else?

A final example: teachers have one of the longest life expectancies of any occupation and, in many cases, will spend more time in retirement than in full-time work. Thanks to pension indexing, many will also collect a pension that ends up being greater than their peak earnings. Once again, taxpayers are forced to backstop these retirement benefits that most private-sector workers could never dream of.

Will the Government Go Broke?

People have told me, *The government will just go broke.* That is not something this author agrees with. Absent severe social unrest, governments don't fold when the math stops working. They change the rules. They raise existing taxes, cut benefits, broaden the tax base, borrow, print, and redefine measures. Once created, many tools that favour governments tend to stay.

In 1917, during WWI, Ottawa introduced The Income War Tax Act[37] to help finance the war effort. It was supposed to be a temporary measure paid for by less than 10 percent of Canadians. Today, we know it as income tax, and it's the core pillar of revenues.

More recently, governments have used financial repression. It involves measures such as interest rate caps, reserve requirements or a tighter association between banks and governments. This allows governments to channel funds from the private sector to themselves. One example, when government borrows at extremely low interest rates, this can result in investors earning less than the rate of inflation, which is repressive. Translation: Savers like you bear the burden and earn negative real returns, and the government's fiscal math looks better, often at the expense of your standard of living.

As we have discussed earlier, Canadians own substantial assets—land, homes, businesses, savings, investments, and pensions. Most are already taxed or regulated, but the search for *new* revenue never stops. Your principal residence is one of the last major asset pools not taxed on a broad basis. It's an easy target, even though most politicians will deny that your home is on their radar. Please ask yourself: would the federal government *go broke* or skip its payroll before taxing your home, or increasing taxes on your other assets or income?

No, your wealth is Ottawa's ongoing backup plan.

Why Investors Should Care:

Jenn crossed her arms. "I'm still stuck on the part where I'm paying for someone else's million-dollar pension top-up, and we don't even get a tax receipt."

Scott agreed. "Yes, government policy choices show up in your life as higher taxes, clawbacks, and rule changes. You also end up with a smaller pool of money compounding at a lower rate."

Pamela leaned back, amused but curious. "Okay, Scott. After all that doom and fiscal gloom … are you seriously saying there's hope?"

Scott replied, "Yes. Individually, we can't control policy, but we can control structure, costs, and our own behaviour. Build for after-tax, after-fee compounding outcomes, and you can outrun a lot of those policy headwinds. Diversify globally and keep a cash buffer so you're never a forced seller on a policy headline."

Lisa chimed in, "You can also maximize your TFSA, right-size your RRSP, and keep portfolio turnover low to minimize current taxes."

"Thanks, Lisa," Scott nodded. "So, collectively, what will our smarter, more prosperous future look like?"

A Golden Future

Scott began, "Canada should be the most prosperous country among peers. We have the resources, the people, and the infrastructure. We just need to stop tripping over our own government."

Pamela raised an eyebrow, "You make that sound easy. Just hit *fix* on decades of bad policy?"

"Not easy," Scott replied. "Give it a decade, and it's doable. We don't need upheaval—just smarter, less ideological governments. Ones that respect taxpayer dollars and treat the word *investment* like it means something and not a euphemism for reckless spending."

Jenn snorted. "Can you tell us how you really feel?"

Scott responded. "Here's a wild idea. Anyone near a government budget and our tax dollars should have to demonstrate proficiency in economic literacy and be accountable for their spending decisions."

Lisa laughed. "What about the red tape?"

Scott chuckled. "Trim the fat, keep safeguards, and technology should simplify, not spawn more forms. Let's use science and evidence, not slogans, to drive policies."

Scott caught his breath. "We also need to stop pretending that government employee pay can keep outpacing private-sector wages. With defined-benefit pensions and richer benefits, total public-sector compensation can be as much as fifty percent higher than in comparable private-sector roles."

Pamela leaned forward. "Speaking of pensions, what about Canada Pension Plan and Old Age Security?"

"OAS is stuck in a 1950s-time warp," Scott said. "It was built for shorter lifespans. We need to adjust eligibility based on income and life expectancy—or it's going to become unsustainable. As for CPP? It's become a large, complex fund with billions in fees every year going to private equity firms, most of which aren't even Canadian. And in-house managers? Some collect seven-figure bonuses even when fund returns are less than their benchmarks.[38] Meanwhile, Norway runs a fund three times the size for less than a quarter of the cost. We can do better."

Lisa cut in, "So where do investments and taxes fit into this sunny vision?"

"That's simple. Raise TFSA limits, the closest thing to a tax haven for average Canadians. Remove taxes on investment fees, cut capital-gains taxes, and turn back the clock on Tax Freedom Day." Scott smiled at Lisa, "And talk to a qualified accountant to ensure your investments are in the optimal mix of taxable and registered accounts to maximize your compounding but minimize your taxation."

Lisa blushed and tilted her head. "So ... what are the big takeaways?

Scott grinned, "Governments have mastered the art of collecting taxes. Now they must master the art of spending it transparently, like responsible adults. That is where your vote comes in. Demand sustainable budgets and simpler rules. Politicians will follow the votes, just like in the late 1990s when Canadians pushed for balanced budgets." He paused. "With the right tax and policy tweaks, we unlock something extraordinary."

Jenn smiled, "You're awfully optimistic. Like what?"

Scott replied, "There are trillions of dollars in Canadian savings and pensions looking for a profitable home. Ironically, much of that money isn't even invested in Canada. The main reason: we need more stable and responsible policies to improve the investment climate. Do that, and we can unleash a wall of capital coming home as we've never seen before. It could create a virtuous circle of new investment options, more wealth, and the funding to raise living standards. That's the future I believe in for Canada."

"I'll vote for that," Pamela smiled. "So, what's next in our wealth literacy journey?"

Scott said, "We've met the three wolves at your door, next up are your inner wolves—your biases and behaviours that can cost more than any tax rate. You don't want to be your own worst enemy!"

"That sounds fun," Lisa exclaimed. "Here's an idea. I'd like to thank everyone and host a dinner party at my place." Everyone nodded.

Scott looked sheepish. "Can you text me your address? I know I was there once during COVID, but ... "

Lisa giggled, "Ahh … I deleted your number."

Scott chuckled, "Same here, figured I'd never see you again."

Jenn rolled her eyes and laughed. "I'll group text everyone. Lisa, tell me what to bring."

CHAPTER 13

The Self-Destruct Button: The Classic Ways Investors Blow Themselves Up

Lisa's apartment smelled like tomatoes, garlic, and the promise of second helpings. A pot murmured on the stove. The dining table with its mismatched chairs was already set. Jenn poured water and folded napkins into triangles that immediately unfolded themselves. Mike wrestled a cork like it owed him money. Pamela was lining up appetizers with the precision of a surgeon.

Phillip leaned in, eyes bright. "One of the guys at work says it's a no-brainer—his advisor told him an easy double or more. Says we need to buy it next week, though."

Jenn remarked, "Classic FOMO. Slap on a *get rich quick* label and hope no one reads the prospectus."

Before anyone could argue about that logic, the doorbell rang. Lisa jumped up, "That'll be Scott."

Scott stepped in with a couple of bottles of red wine and a shy grin. "Apologies, it took me forever to find wines that pair well with pasta and hard truths."

"They're perfect, but we've already started with the first bottle," Lisa giggled.

Scott looked around the room. "It's nice to see everyone together for a change."

Phillip smirked, "I only came because I love Lisa's cooking."

Pamela frowned, setting down caprese skewers and a small charcuterie board between the wine glasses. She cleared her throat. "And the real reason we are here, Phillip?"

Phillip winced. "Alright, I made a few bad calls, trading stock options and listening to my neighbour's hot stock tip."

Pamela glanced at her husband and then winked at Scott. "And someone finally listened when I suggested he might still have a few things to learn about investing, so here we are."

Scott chuckled, "Well, let's count that as the classic, *don't tell anyone* stock tip. This one brought to you by the neighbour's father-in-law's investment club. Sounds like the tail end of the classic pump-and-dump scheme."

Phillip took on a serious look. "Well, I will admit I learned an expensive lesson, but it has opened my eyes a bit wider and makes me wonder what else I've been wrong about." He looked at Scott. "So, what's on the menu for tonight?"

Scott replied, "Your inner wolves, emotions, and myths."

Jenn smiled. "Sounds yummy, let's dive right in."

The Emotional Minefield

"To invest successfully over a lifetime does not require a stratospheric IQ, unusual business insights or inside information; what is needed is a sound intellectual framework for making decisions and the ability to keep emotions from eroding that framework."
—Warren Buffet

We have all been blessed with a splendid mix of over twenty-five emotions. When it comes to your money, the Big 3 are greed, fear, and hope. These, mixed with ignorance, can form a potent cocktail that runs counter to what it takes for you to be a successful long-term investor.

Your emotions often trigger mental biases that override rational judgment and sabotage performance. To add insult to injury, the investment industry also knows how to exploit these vulnerabilities, selling you overpriced solutions that prey on your fears and inexperience while feeding their own greed-driven interests. Understanding these traps is the first step toward avoiding them.

Greed is Not Always Good

Greed is the disordered desire for more than is fair or deserved. Historically, greed has sometimes fueled progress—driving exploration, innovation, and economic growth, but when it comes to investing, it can have a dangerous dark side. As the old saying goes, "Pigs get fat, hogs get slaughtered." Making a healthy profit is good. Chasing ever-higher returns without discipline is not.

Excessive greed pushes us to act recklessly, ignore warning signs, and ultimately invite ruin. It blinds us to the reality that markets are cyclical, that no asset class stays hot forever, and that chasing the next big thing usually ends with a painful crash.

Fear is a Four-Letter Word

Fear, at its best, is a survival tool and is meant to heighten caution, not halt progress. In investing, fear often backfires, and instead of encouraging smart risk management, it pushes you to take too little risk—or worse, freeze entirely. This fear-driven inertia often leads to poorly diversified portfolios that underperform over time, and you failing to meet long-term goals. In the end, fear doesn't remove risk, it just guarantees missed opportunities.

Hope Is Not a Strategy

Hope is a longing for a specific outcome, but it rarely produces investment results. It's fine to keep your hopes on non-financial outcomes that are out of your control, such as *hoping* your favourite sports team wins a championship, but it can be detrimental to your financial health to hope your portfolio recovers without a plan.

Ignorance Can Be Bliss, But It Can Also Be The Kiss Of Death For Your Portfolio

Ignorance is simply a lack of knowledge, education, or awareness. All of which are essential elements to being a successful long-term investor. In finance, not understanding the basics can leave you wide open to costly mistakes. As the old saying goes, "A fool and his money are soon parted."

Scott stated, "In short, unchecked emotions and ignorance can press that self-destruct button for us."

Jenn asked, "So, how do we keep from pressing it?"

Scott answered, "First, recognize that ignorance and emotion blind you to risk—and that blindness is its own form of wealth sabotage. Let's shine a light on the risks so you can see them coming."

Risk: The Silent Shadow That Follows Every Investment

"There is nothing wrong with taking calculated risks. That is quite different from being rash."
—General George S. Patton

Risk is simply the potential for harm or financial loss. It is also unavoidable and present in every decision, every investment, and every market.

Risk is subjective, so what feels reckless to one person might seem perfectly reasonable to another. Your goals, time horizon, and your emotional wiring all play a role in how you perceive danger—and whether you react wisely, foolishly, or somewhere in between.

When most people think of risk, they picture a scary, flashing-red moment when their investments shrink on paper. That's real. But it's far from the only danger. There are three broad categories of risk that quietly stalk even the best-laid financial plans.

Market-Related Risks: These are the risks most investors think about—interest rate spikes, liquidity crunches, valuation bubbles, sudden volatility, or too much money tied up in one area (concentration risk). Smart diversification and keeping enough cash on hand can help you ride out market storms without being forced to sell when prices are at their worst.

Behavioural and Personal Risks: These risks tend to come from inside our own heads. FOMO (fear of missing out), over-diversification, bad advice, and even outright fraud all prey on human psychology. A written financial plan—and regular, unemotional check-ins—are the best antidote to panic selling, impulse buying, and other self-sabotaging moves.

Structural and External Risks: Sometimes, the hidden dangers come from the systems and people you trust. Credit downgrades, economic shocks, flawed financial models, or even mistakes by your fund manager can all inflict damage beneath the surface. Protect yourself with thorough due diligence, low-cost investment options, and always maintain a margin of safety.

Ironically, you often have the most money at stake right before or during retirement, precisely when a major error can be catastrophic. A little preparation now, beats scrambling for a lifeline later. For example, you could start by creating guardrails and rules with strategies such as position sizing, holding a cash buffer, or setting rebalancing bands that will help you avoid extreme blow-ups.

How I Made My Fortune

"It was really quite simple. I bought an apple for $0.05, spent the evening polishing it and sold it the next day for $0.10.
With this, I bought two apples and spent the evening polishing them and sold them for $0.20, and so it went until I had amassed $1.60.
It was then that my wife's father died and left us $1 million."
— Anonymous Entrepreneur

Most of us don't have a rich family member to catapult us into the millionaires' club. You might have diligently saved for decades, built and sold a successful business, gotten lucky with a couple of stock picks, or lived near Ottawa and *won* fat government consulting contracts. Not to dismiss your efforts if you earned your million honestly, but I'm afraid that is the easy part.

Keeping your nest egg is the tough part! Emotions, biases, poor decision-making, and other personal or social influences, combined with an ever-shifting market and economic environment, create countless ways to *blow yourself up*. Let's take a careful walk through this minefield and ensure you don't become your own worst enemy.

Psychological and Emotional Traps That Blow Up Your Returns

The smartest investors fall victim to common mental traps that quietly sabotage their results. A few of the most dangerous include:

Overconfidence: Overestimating your skills can lead to excessive risk-taking—and often to painful losses.

Loss Aversion: Investors hate losing money more than they love making it, which often causes them to sell winning investments too early while clinging to losers too long.

Herd Mentality: Charles Mackay may have said it best, "Men, it has been well said, think in herds; it will be seen that they go mad in herds, while they only recover their senses slowly, and one by one." Following the crowd into bubbles or panicked selloffs usually ends badly. What feels safe in a crowd is often financially disastrous.

Recency Bias: Fixating on the latest market moves instead of thinking long-term leads to shortsighted decisions that miss the bigger picture.

Anchoring: Getting emotionally attached to your original purchase price can blind you to changing realities, causing you to hold bad investments for too long.

Scott paused, "I probably shouldn't tell you this, but I have my own greed and overconfidence tale. It's a true story about how I blew a huge hole in my family's finances."

Mike chuckled, "I knew you weren't telling us something. Let's hear it." Everyone laughed.

"Over the years, I would sometimes sell put options, which is a common trading strategy," Scott said.

Jenn smiled, "In English, please."

Scott grinned. "When you sell a put, the buyer pays you a premium for the right—during a set period—to sell you shares at a preset price (the strike). If the share price stays above the strike, you keep the premium, kind of like a free lunch."

Phillip's eyes lit up. "That sounds great. Maybe I should try it."

Scott looked at Phillip, "Or maybe not. The catch is that if the stock price drops below the strike, you're obligated to buy the shares at the higher strike price. Another catch is that the premiums are usually small, but the losses can be large, as we will soon find out."

Scott continued, "My blow-up involved the shares of BCE (Bell Canada). In 2008, the Ontario Teachers' Pension Plan (OTPP) had offered to pay $42.75 per BCE share in a leveraged buyout. It seemed like a no-brainer; I got overconfident and greedy and sold far too many put options. I was focused on the thousands of dollars in premium income, blinding me to the potential downside risks."

"I conveniently ignored what could go wrong. BCE was solid, and OTPP had extremely deep pockets."

Pamela sat forward, "So what happened?"

"It was November 26, 2008. I was with my family at Disneyland, the *happiest place on earth*. My young son was tired, so I took him back to the hotel. I turned on the TV to the big news of the day, OTPP had found a loophole and the buyout of BCE might fail. BCE stock was cratering. The day before, it had closed at $38.35, and now it was trading at $24 per share. The puts I had sold flipped from *income* to *obligation* and had blown an instant $200,000 plus hole in my family's accounts."

Lisa's eyes widened, "What did you do?"

Scott chuckled, "The first thing I did was sit down and take a lot of deep breaths. After that, I refused to panic and continued pretending I was in the happiest place on earth. Once we got back home to Canada, I used my home line of credit to get our investment accounts back onside and then started a series of *repair trades* that took about two years to unwind the mess I had created. The good news: BCE recovered, and we ended up in the black, but not without a lot of stress and me eating a ton of humble pie."

Mike grinned, "So what lessons did you learn?"

"Good question. First, BCE hadn't traded below $30 in about two years, so I thought that was a pretty good floor for the stock price. I was wrong. Secondly, the Global Financial Crisis happened, which changed the market's and OTPP's appetite for risk, so the sure-thing deal died. Lastly, besides being rash, greedy and overconfident, I had forgotten to ask myself one thing."

Jenn uttered, "Which was?"

Scott responded, "What will the consequences be if I am wrong? In this case, I hadn't priced my potential exposure in dollars or considered the grief it could cause. It was not fun."

"Thanks for sharing that story," Jenn commented. "I know it's important to recognize mental traps ahead of time, but I noted you kept your cool when things seemed to be blowing up around you."

"Yes, a great observation," Scott complimented Jenn. "Not panicking is one of the essential keys to your long-term success as an investor. Whether it's a mistake you make, or the next time the market has one of its regular downward episodes, you must acknowledge you will face some stressful times."

Decision Downfalls

Successful investing isn't just about what you buy, it's about how you think. A lack of education and a refusal to understand what you own, plus placing blind trust in advisors and experts, is an invitation to trouble. Other dangerous decision-making pitfalls include:

Believing Overly Optimistic Projections: When future returns sound too good to be true, they usually are.

Confirmation Bias: We naturally seek out information that agrees with what we already believe—ignoring critical facts that might challenge our assumptions.

Naïve Reinforcement: Mistaking lucky outcomes for skill can create false confidence and bad habits, often leading to bigger mistakes later.

Extrapolation: Assuming that recent performance trends will continue forever fuels reckless decisions and often causes panic selling during downturns and blind buying during booms.

Narrow Framing: Focusing too narrowly on one investment, metric, or moment blinds you to the bigger picture and weakens your strategy.

Market Timing: Famed investor Peter Lynch said it best, "Far more money has been lost by investors preparing for corrections, or trying to anticipate corrections, than has been lost in corrections themselves."

Trying to predict the best times to exit and re-enter markets is a fool's game.

Recognizing these common downfalls and building a disciplined, thoughtful process with consistent rules can mean the difference between lasting success and financial heartbreak.

Money Behaviours That Drain Your Wealth

"Annual income twenty pounds, annual expenditure nineteen, nineteen and six, result happiness.
Annual income twenty pounds, annual expenditure twenty pounds ought and six, result misery."
— Charles Dickens, *David Copperfield*, 1850

Living beyond your means is probably the single biggest behavioural culprit in sabotaging your wealth. Other common pitfalls include treating investing like gambling, using excessive leverage, and chasing get-rich-quick schemes. Impatience will also undermine your wealth.

Bad habits such as selling winners and retaining losers (the disposition effect), trading too often, poor position sizing, or using the gambler's *double or nothing* strategy—where a player doubles the bet to erase the debt if they win, but owes twice as much if they lose—can dig an even deeper hole.

Lastly, be wary if your advisor recommends that you borrow money to *leverage up* your portfolio. While your account balance will appear larger, so will their management fees. You'll also pay interest on the borrowed funds and carry a higher-risk portfolio. Leverage magnifies both gains and losses—meaning a market downturn can wipe out years of gains far faster than you expect, and in extreme cases, leave you owing more than your initial investment.

Personal Circumstances and Social Influences

The best financial plan can be undone by forces both in and out of your control. Unqualified advice, such as that from well-meaning relatives, friends, or casual cocktail party chatter can lead to disastrous decisions if you don't apply proper skepticism. In addition, lending money to family members or friends without clear terms and due diligence often turns good intentions into pain, both personal and economic.

Major life events like divorce, illness, or sudden job loss can also derail finances if you're unprepared. In the longer term, failing to account for the true costs of aging, especially given the rising burdens of health care, can lead to money death, also known as the moment you outlive your assets.

Lastly, please remember that plain old luck lurks everywhere in investing. Bad luck tends to strike hardest when all your eggs are in one basket and the handle breaks. Just as important, never confuse good luck with skill—because the market has a way of reminding us of which is which.

The Behaviour Gap: How Emotions Slash Returns

Poor decision-making—fueled by the mental shortcuts, emotional impulses and our lack of risk awareness—often creates a *Behaviour Gap.* This occurs when the returns you earn fall far short of their potential. Several studies have illustrated that, on average; many investors pocket only a fraction of their funds' published returns because of bad timing and churn.

A famous illustration is the Magellan Fund run by Peter Lynch[39]. It soared at an average 29.2% annual rate of return from 1977 to 1990, and despite this extremely impressive performance, legend has it that the average unitholder's return was said to be closer to 7%. In dollar terms, $1,000 at the fund's reported rate of return would have grown to $27,390, while the average investor's supposed outcome was closer to $2,410. This $25,000 gap was driven by *bad behaviour,* not markets. Even if the story is not entirely true, its lessons hold up well: impatience, excessive trading, and poor market timing (ill-timed withdrawals after drops and late re-entries into the market that missed recoveries) can severely undermine your results.

Jenn set down her glass and laughed softly. "That is a lot of ways to blow our portfolio up! You know what? I came here ready to fire my bank, but I didn't realize I also needed to fire my brain! Our talk gives me hope though".

Scott stated, "All of us are susceptible to irrelevant influences from our brains and our environment. The good news is that we can turn these potential mistakes into opportunities. For example, we could develop new strategies or use new tools such as simple investment guidelines that help us make better decisions."

Lisa responded. "So, if I heard you correctly: emotions drive outcomes, risk is everywhere, and behaviours can matter more than markets or fees. You keep more when rules—not moods—run your money."

"Yes," Scott agreed. "Otherwise, it's like walking in front of a steam roller to pick up dimes and nickels while $20 dollar bills are on the sidewalk for the taking."

Pamela nodded and looked at her husband. "For Phillip and me, step one is to stop procrastinating and to put guardrails in place now. Apathy and undisciplined investing have cost us dearly."

Scott raised his glass. "Great first step, Pamela, and another part of Wealth Literacy—understanding how money works in the real world, and how you work around money. Nail that, and you'll disarm the self-destruct button in no time. Next up: Myths & Realities, what you think is true, but isn't, and what it's costing you."

Lisa glanced towards the kitchen and then back at the table. "Alright," she said, and smiled at Scott as she stood. "Appetizers are over. Time for the main course!"

CHAPTER 14

Myths and Realities: Pretty Stories, Sharper Teeth, Uglier Outcomes

Mike and Phillip were clearing the appetizer plates just as Lisa returned from the kitchen with a massive dish of steaming pasta, setting it down with a satisfied sigh. "Dinner is served!"

Scott followed her lead with a tray of fresh, hot garlic bread from the oven and sat down. "This next bit is spicy. You've heard the blowups, now we're into the myths—why they feel safe and why they quietly cost you."

Scott tapped his notebook. "Here's the rule for tonight: *myths feel good; evidence makes money.*"

Pamela smiled. "So, believing the story is more comfortable than checking the math?"

Scott responded. "Yes. Comfort sells, but it's a cost center. When you face adversity in investing, you make changes based on facts, not on fear or any other emotion. Let's look at some of the common stories that drain returns."

Financial Urban Legends: The Top Myths Quietly Costing You

A lot of what you hear about money and investing is outdated, misleading, or just wrong. While some myths are harmless, others are not, but they can all chip away at your time, your money, and your trust.

Let's start by putting some common financial planning myths

under the bright lights and matching each one with a testable reality. With this, you can challenge bad assumptions, dodge common traps, and take more control of your next move.

Myth: You Don't Need a Financial Plan.

Reality: Without a plan, you're financially adrift. It is your road map to long-term success and shouldn't be considered optional. Households with financial plans are two times more likely to save enough for retirement. Individuals with financial plans also feel 83% more confident about their finances after just one year, and they make smarter decisions, have better relationships not only with their money, but also other people. Even a short, written plan is better than "I have it in my head."

Myth: Financial Planning is Only About Retirement.

Reality: Retirement is only one part of financial planning. Effective planning covers and coordinates multiple areas—budgeting, tax strategy, insurance, debt, education savings, estate planning and risk mitigation—so every decision works together. Sadly, many younger households skip planning and miss a great opportunity to start early.

Myth: A Budget is the Same as a Financial Plan.

Reality: Your budget tracks what happens today, so do it. Your plan directs tomorrow—contributions, asset mix, taxation and what you'll do when markets zig, and then zag. It is the map for building wealth and your long-term financial security.

Myth: Financial Planning is too Expensive or Complicated.

Reality: The financial industry benefits from making planning seem complicated—pushing high-fee advisors and complex products that make them more money, not you. However, starting with a basic written plan, low-cost investments and periodic check-ups costs little. It's also superior to an outright neglect of planning, which often ends up costing you far more in missed opportunities and expensive mistakes over the long run. More good news, modern tools and technology have also made financial planning less intimidating and more cost-effective than in previous years.

Myth: Financial Planning is Only for the Wealthy.

Reality: Everyone benefits from planning, and regardless of income level, it is your foundation for financial health. Effective planning empowers you to grow your wealth, achieve goals, and manage risks more effectively. Wealth follows planning, not the other way around.

Pamela sat forward, "People often act like they only need a plan once they're in trouble."

Scott nodded. "Sometimes that's true, but the edge is to plan before trouble and keep the plan alive. The bigger mistake is treating your plan as a set-and-forget document."

Lisa smiled, "It's the same thing I tell my business clients —we adjust the plan when life changes."

Jenn tilted her head. "So, what's the rule?"

Scott said, "Update your financial plan when there are major life changes such as a birth, death, marriage, job change, move, major purchase, or big market fluctuations. That's when you need to review goals, funding, and risks. That habit will be your edge."

He glanced around the table, "Alright, let's cue up the investing myths."

Myth: Investing is the Same as Gambling.

Reality: Gambling is pure chance with negative expected value, meaning the odds are that you will lose some, if not all your money. Investing, on the other hand, is deliberate and based on strategy, discipline, and informed decision-making to achieve long-term growth. A well-researched and diversified investment plan increases your odds of long-term success and boosts your wealth. If you're looking for thrills, stick to the blackjack table—not your retirement account.

Myth: Past Performance Predicts Future Results.

Reality: Past results don't forecast tomorrow's winners or losers. Markets evolve, leadership rotates, and conditions shift. Nortel, a market darling of the late 1990s, is a cautionary tale. Its share price surged, then collapsed to pennies, and the company ultimately went bankrupt, wiping out investors who extrapolated yesterday's gains into tomorrow's riches. Don't chase yesterday's winners, diversify, and follow rebalancing rules.

Myth: You Need to Time the Market to Win.

Reality: Even seasoned professionals rarely get market timing right. Timing the market requires you to be correct twice—when to get in, and when to get out. For example, during the COVID crash in 2020, we had two clients who timed their exit from stock markets almost perfectly and avoided the bulk of the ensuing declines in February and March of 2020. For a short while, I was impressed by their apparent acumen. Meanwhile, for all other clients, we rebalanced their portfolios into cheaper equities. Patience paid off, and within a year, those clients who stayed invested had fully recovered their paper losses, and then some. The ones who tried to time the bottom? They couldn't muster up the conviction to re-enter the market and they missed one of the fastest rebounds in history. A year later they had earned next to nothing in cash, still underwater. The truth? Time in the market beats timing the market almost always.

Myth: Bonds are Safe.

Reality: Yes, bonds are generally considered safer and less volatile than stocks, but that doesn't mean they're risk-free. For example, during the 2022 mini-bond market crash, many so-called safe bond funds experienced double-digit declines,[40] showing that *safe* can still hurt your account balance. Investors also need to know that GICs and bonds are not the same, though both can play an important part in a diversified portfolio.

GICs (Guaranteed Investment Certificates) are deposit products. Your principal and stated interest rate are guaranteed if held to maturity, and eligible deposits are insured through Canada Deposit Insurance Corporation (CDIC) to a limit of $100,000 at member financial institutions. GICs have little to no price volatility and are usually locked in, so early redemptions are usually restricted or penalized.

Bonds are marketable securities and are not insured. You can buy bonds as new issues or purchase and sell them on the secondary market anytime before their maturity. A bond's price can fluctuate depending on the issuer's health (credit risk) and interest rate movements (duration risk). Because of this, a bond may trade above or below its par value (par value is the nominal value stated on a bond certificate, typically in multiples of $1,000). The easiest way to remember how a bond changes price is to think of a teeter-totter. If interest rates go up, a bond's price will go down, and vice versa.

Two Rules of Thumb: Depending upon market conditions and interest rate movements, bonds may offer higher yields than GICs. When buying fixed income, it is prudent to compare both bonds and GICs with similar maturities to maximize your returns. Secondly, be sure to match your term or maturity to your needs (i.e. match your assets to your liabilities). For example, you might use insured GICs for near-term cash goals and high-quality bonds in a diversified portfolio for medium- to long-term investment horizons, seeking income and potential capital gains.

Myth: High Fees Mean Better Performance.

Reality: This is one of the industry's favourite fairy tales. Fees are one risk you have full control over. Lower-cost index funds consistently outperform high-fee actively managed funds over time because those high fees quietly compound against you, eroding your share of market returns and becoming one of the biggest obstacles to your success. Pay less and keep more.

Phillip inquired, "So, is that it for the myths, or are there more I should be worried about?"

Scott elaborated, "Plenty more. Like the idea that you must pay off all your debts before you invest a dime. Just be sure you pay off high-interest debt, like credit cards, first."

Jenn raised an eyebrow. "And let me guess, people also think the market only goes up?"

Scott chuckled, "That and thinking a couple of hot stock picks will beat diversification. Spoiler, it doesn't."

Pamela asked, "And people actually believe all that?"

Scott responded, "We all have at some point, it's human nature. But here's the thing—these myths didn't come from nowhere. They were shaped, packaged and sold by the very industry that says it's helping you. When something doesn't sound right, be skeptical, and check the facts before you commit any money."

Scott put his fork down. "While we are on the topic of myths, there's an increasingly controversial area that sometimes blurs into fantasy, we call it ESG."

Phillip smirked, "Does that stand for Everything Sounds Good?"

Pamela rolled her eyes, and everyone laughed.

CHAPTER 15

ESG: Friend, Foe, or a Wolf in Green Clothing?

Lisa's eyes widened, "Is that really what it means?"

Jenn chuckled. "It means Environmental, Social and Governance."

Lisa replied, "Oh, I've heard that term before, but mostly in connection to climate change. There's a lot of talk about carbon dioxide, global warming, and the end of the world. It all sounds complicated."

Jenn nodded. "Exactly. That's why it's sometimes hard to take it seriously when people try to reduce it to a single score or a checkbox."

Scott leaned forward, intrigued. "Is there something you are not telling us? I get the feeling you are speaking from experience."

Jenn gave him a wry smile, "I did a minor in Environmental Science—real environmental science. And believe me, some of what gets passed off as climate policy these days is just a hodge podge of good intentions, marketing spin, and half-baked data."

Lisa stammered. "So ... what is ESG exactly?"

Scott stated, "The E, environment, focuses on conservation of the natural world and covers emissions from carbon dioxide or CO_2, other gases, air and water pollution, climate change, biodiversity, deforestation, energy efficiency, waste management and water scarcity, among others."

Jenn, energized, jumped in. "The S, social, focuses on people and relationships and includes factors like gender and diversity, employee engagement, community, human rights, labour standards and customer data protection. Lastly, the G, governance, includes factors such as company board composition and executive compensation, accounting standards, bribery and corruption, and lobbying. Basically, how a company is supposed to run itself."

Phillip squinted. "So, we're talking about three massive buckets of almost every major issue on earth, but what does it have to do with my investments?"

Scott shrugged. "Good question. Politicians, regulators and some investors, are pushing companies to standardize and disclose all this stuff. It's increasingly becoming part of how risk and opportunity are evaluated, and that can affect the value of your investments. For your portfolio, ESG can change how much you pay for investment management, as well as how your holdings may differ in comparison to the overall market and how that may affect your investment returns."

Lisa smiled. "Okay, the accountant in me is finally starting to get it."

Jenn set down her mug. "Let's not forget that not everybody in the ESG space is here to save the planet. Some are just looking to cash in while pretending they care."

Mike grumbled, "So, we're saving the world and sometimes getting scammed. Great."

Scott responded, "Yes, there are plenty of voices in the ESG space, many with different goals. And yes, some are just trying to fill their pockets by shoving the world into three buckets."

Jenn smirked. "Sure. Just promise I don't need to buy carbon credits by the end. Maybe tell us the story about the Great Smog of London, if you know what that is!"

Scott exclaimed, "As a matter of fact I do!"

ESG is Born

"It was December 4, 1952. A high-pressure air mass stalled over the Thames River Valley in England."

Lisa looked up, "Is this a true story?"

"Very real," Scott said. "The cold air swept in from the west, trapping frigid temperatures and pollutants in place. Smoke, soot and sulphur dioxide from the area's industries, cars and residents burning coal mixed with thick fog to create a lethal smog. It cast a visible pall over hundreds of square miles, and within two days, virtually all sunlight was gone, and visibility was reduced to just five yards."

Scott continued. "They called it the Great Smog of London.[41] People and animals literally could not breathe; thousands of people and animals died, many suffocating in their sleep."

Pamela looked stunned. "That's horrifying. I had no idea something like that had happened."

"Most people don't. The 'Big Smoke' triggered the UK to pass the Clean Air Act in 1956, a landmark environmental law."

Lisa sighed, "It's a sad part of human nature that it often requires disaster to create positive changes."

The Promise of ESG

Most of us want a society that treats people fairly with dignity and adequate housing, where we can breathe clean air and drink safe water, and where corporations act responsibly towards both the environment and their stakeholders. At its best, Environmental, Social, and Governance (ESG) investing seeks to promote those ideals, and can provide a framework for businesses to be accountable not just for profit, but for their impact on people and the planet.

This is the promise of ESG, a future in which companies are incentivized to act ethically, sustainably, and transparently, creating long-term value not only for shareholders but for the whole society. ESG aims to embed these considerations into how businesses operate and how investors assess risk and opportunity.

However, ideals work best when evaluated. That is why it is essential to evaluate ESG critically, watching where the money flows, questioning who sets the rules, and remaining skeptical of blanket claims. When applied thoughtfully, ESG can be a powerful tool for accountability, sustainability, and a better society.

Of the three pillars, governance is currently the most robust. It has been shaped by decades of financial scandals—from Enron to WorldCom—that exposed the consequences of weak oversight and opaque decision-making. In contrast, the environmental and social components are less regulated, and more vulnerable to interpretation, misuse, or outright manipulation. If, and when, the E and S pillars are grounded in more comparable metrics and honestly presented cost-benefit trade-offs, they could sharpen risk assessments, and that would better align portfolios with investors' goals.

Why Investors Should Care

The body of knowledge surrounding ESG is vast, and you need to know that ESG has the potential to reshape capital markets, policy, and society in ways that may not be supportive of your financial health. While many environmental and social advocates are driven by good intentions, ESG has fueled what may be the largest financial gold rush of all time. Around the products sits an ecosystem—consultants, data vendors, auditors, certifiers, regulators and government departments—each taking a cut through compliance systems, government subsidies, certifications, and advisory services.

An expensive taxpayer-funded example was the Sustainable Development Technology Canada (SDTC) program, which was supposed to provide funding to support the development of innovative technologies that promote sustainable development. A detailed Auditor General of Canada report found dozens of conflict-of-interest policy breaches and tens of millions in funding steered toward projects that materially overstated the actual benefits of their environmental impacts. Sadly, instead of fixing root causes and enforcing accountability, the federal government simply closed the fund and shifted its mandate to the National Research Council of Canada, with taxpayers footing the bill and little to show.

The above example also illustrates why investors, voters, and taxpayers all need to recognize that an increasing number of ESG *leaders* and commentators approach complex environmental challenges with wishful thinking, as opposed to grounding ESG in scientific and engineering knowledge. Aspirational goals, such as *net zero* emissions or fully circular economies, must be assessed against both economic trade-offs and real-world physical constraints.

Otherwise, we risk trying to implement ESG policies that run counter to the reality of the physical world we all live in. It will also create the formula for disillusionment, misallocation of capital, new taxes, a lower standard of living, and ultimately, failure. Conversely, if policies are rooted in sound science, comparable metrics, and independent verification, ESG initiatives can reduce risk and catalyze practical innovation.

The Financial Institutions' Perspective and the Commercialization of ESG

Financial institutions increasingly integrate ESG factors into their investment strategies, in part because companies with strong ESG performance are believed to deliver long-term value and be more resilient to environmental and social risks. Done properly, this is true.

Scott looked up from his notes. "That's the theory, anyway."

Pamela asked, "And the practice?"

"Less noble. More ... monetized," Scott quipped.

While ESG began as a framework for ethical investing, its commercial potential has quickly taken centre stage. Today, ESG has become a sprawling profit engine, creating new streams of fees, taxes, compliance and government control. Most companies disclose selectively—whether in annual reports or separate sustainability documents—but the data remains voluntary, and ESG metrics are still not standardized. Institutions like the International Financial Reporting Standards (IFRS) are working to fix that, but progress is slow, and comparability is still limited and often subjective.

Scott nodded. "A few years back, ESG mutual funds became another *flavour of the month* and many shot to the top of the performance charts. In hindsight, this outperformance was driven more by sector tilts and an investor stampede into these funds, rather than the stock-picking skill of ESG fund managers. Predictably, our old friend, *reversion to the mean*, kicked in, and many of the funds came back down to earth with a thud. Investors have realized ESG still requires proper due diligence, like all investments."

Pamela sat up, "So, over the longer term, what does this mean?"

Scott said, "For many ESG funds, you can expect broad market-like returns, adjusted for your ESG sector tilts, less any ESG fee premiums, which are typically in the 0.25 % range."

He added, "Keep a balanced view. ESG concepts aren't meaningless, but nor are they especially new in many cases. Capable analysts have considered environmental, social, and governance risks long before the acronym ESG existed, just under different names. For example, the fact that a mining company ignoring environmental laws or labour standards might end up facing higher legal and operational risks that affect share prices negatively is hardly a new insight."

Scott noted, "ESG can add value if you ask the right questions up front." He ticked them off on his fingers.

1. What exactly are they measuring? Specifics or just a generic *sustainability* score?
2. Who is verifying it? Is there an independent audit, or is it self-re-

ported by the company or fund?

3. How transparent is it? Can you see the full holdings list and the scoring methodology?
4. What is the track record, or is it a rebranded product?
5. What is the cost premium? And if so, is the impact worth the difference?

When Good Intentions Get (Extraordinarily) Expensive

Governments across the globe have pledged trillions of dollars to fund environmental cleanups, to promote equity and inclusion, and implement regulatory mandates. The largest line item is the transition to net-zero, a number some have pegged at roughly $275 trillion (USD)[42] in cumulative investment by 2050. This figure is equal to approximately half the world's net worth circa 2025.

Lisa chortled. "Two hundred and seventy-five trillion? That's not even a real number."

Scott paused. "For perspective, that's roughly twenty times the $18.4 trillion (CDN) net worth of all Canadians. Even if we donated everything, it would barely move the needle."

Pamela asked, "Where does government policy fit?"

Scott replied, "Cleaning up our environment and managing transition risks can be real positives for all of us. The danger is when governments use our money without our permission to pursue broad policy goals without clear mandates or provable outcomes."

Scott added, "ESG implemented pragmatically could definitely be a boon to our society, living standards and quality of life. Unfortunately, if it's hijacked by bankers and government officials laying out their grand vision for a *brave new future* driven by ideology and self-interest, it could become costly with little to show."

Phillip looked a bit puzzled, then gave a small, wry smile. "So, the worst case is the limo-and-private-jet crowd spends our money at climate summits—then sells us austerity, with a side of crickets?"

A beat of silence. Mike raised an eyebrow. "So ... what's for dessert?"

CHAPTER 16

Overwhelmed to Informed: Wealth Literacy That Works Even When Markets Don't

Lisa returned from the kitchen with a tray of homemade salted-caramel cheesecake slices.

Phillip grinned, "Each one of those looks like a plated banker's overpromise—drizzled, gleaming, and impossible to resist."

Jenn's eyes doubled in size. "I already hate how much I love this."

Mike looked at his wife and laughed. "So … the perfect metaphor for the next topic?"

Scott chuckled. "Exactly. Welcome to dessert—the financial version of I know I shouldn't, but I can't help myself."

Scott paused. "Speaking of helping ourselves, who here, other than Phillip, spends more than one hour per month reviewing your accounts or educating yourself on your financial affairs?"

Everybody sat quietly.

Finally, Jenn spoke softly. "I must confess that I spend very little time on my finances; that's why we have financial advisors."

Scott nodded. "That's exactly how the system likes it—you trust, you don't look closely, and you pay for it."

Lisa sighed, "Feels about right."

Scott replied, "And there's another catch; when you outsource the method, you outsource a piece of your confidence. Tonight, we change that."

Scott stated, "We've looked at ways we blow ourselves up, now let's turn that around and look at how you can arm yourselves with the confidence you need to level the playing field with your financial services providers. I touched on it briefly earlier in our chats, but now we're going to take a much closer look at Financial Literacy 2.0, or what I prefer to call Wealth Literacy."

Pamela smiled, "Speaking for all of us, I know we want to feel more confident and in control. Please point us in the right direction."

Wealth Literacy: Your Best Ally

"An investment in knowledge pays the best interest."
—Benjamin Franklin

One of the biggest shortfalls of Canada's educational system is how little emphasis it places on financial or wealth literacy. When I was in high school, I learned how to calculate the volume of a cone and how to dissect a frog, but no one explained how credit card interest worked—or that bank advisors aren't required to put your best interests first. As a result, many young Canadians graduate without basic money skills—even though in today's society's financial literacy should rank right alongside English and math as a life essential.

A strong financial education would include understanding how to budget, manage debt, navigate taxation, plan for education and retirement needs, and build basic investing skills. Imagine if teenagers graduated understanding how the Canadian financial system works, recognized how government spending and taxes affect their future, and were prepared for major milestones like buying a home. They would know how to navigate day-to-day financial realities, such as mortgages and credit cards, or how to spot the true costs hidden inside financial products.

They would also discern the difference between investing and speculating and know how our own psychology shapes our money decisions. Just as we're expected to be informed voters, we can, and should be, informed economic participants, strengthening both our personal finances and Canada's overall prosperity.

Same tokens, different odds.

Jenn exhaled. "We never talked about money at home. I just absorbed what I saw, and the message was, 'Don't worry, the bank will help.'"

Mike nodded. "Same. RRSP season, then silence."

Scott said, "That's common. If schools don't teach it, the industry will fill the gap with marketing, and too many people end up paying more for products they don't need."

Jenn groaned, "What about those *free* seminars?"

"Mostly sales pitches," Scott noted.

Jenn joked. "I wish you'd told me that earlier. It would've saved me from a few flavour-of-the-month funds."

Scott chuckled. "Exactly! And the first tool to increase your wealth literacy is numeracy—so you can spot costs, compare options, and keep more of your money."

Numeracy: Your Secret Weapon

Numeracy is the ability to use numbers to solve problems, spot patterns, and make logical choices. It also lets you price the future cost of today's decisions. These skills are a core pillar of financial literacy. Over the years, I have seen clients, colleagues, and even industry veterans fall prey to confusion about common areas like percentages, fees, interest rates, or how compounding works.

Studies have shown that approximately half of Canadians struggle with basic math, making most money topics, such as mortgages, interest rates and investment fees, difficult to grasp. Strengthening your numeracy doesn't require a math degree. It just means becoming comfortable enough with numbers to spot hidden costs, negotiate better terms, and avoid falling for financial products that look good on paper but collapse under scrutiny. Improving your numeracy is a controllable, high-impact way to keep more of your money working for you, not for others.

Along with numeracy, I would add economic literacy. It is the ability to understand and interpret basic economic concepts and is another practical edge for your personal finances. Improved economic literacy would also help create more productive and pragmatic public dialogue about government policies and their trade-offs. Instead, many of these debates have become increasingly driven by narratives and schemes which are not self-sustaining without taxpayers' money and don't offer a path to constructive solutions for our society.

Focus on What You Can Control

You have more control over your financial situation than you think, and a reasonable level of wealth literacy gives you the necessary skill set to recognize what you can and cannot control. For example, you have the power to choose whether you seek professional advice, what you are willing to pay, and who you hire by assessing an advisor's experience, qualifications, level of independence and objectivity. You can also control your own discipline, your mindset, and create practical financial and investment plans. They needn't be elaborate, just realistic for your short-term and long-term financial goals and achievable within the effort and time you are willing to invest.

On the other hand, no one—not you, not your advisor, not even the experts on TV—can control market fluctuations, economic cycles, interest rates, inflation, or sudden shocks to individual companies. Fortunately, greater wealth literacy empowers you to recognize these risks early, prepare accordingly, and make smarter, calmer decisions when they inevitably arise.

For example, in 2020, bond yields sank below 1% as the world scrambled through the pandemic. Yet many *Big Bank* bond funds still charged more than 1 % in management fees—upside down math and an opportune time to re-evaluate or even sell these investments.

Jenn pushed her plate aside. "So, wait—are you saying some investments were paying less than their fees?"

"Exactly," Scott said. "Yields under 1 %, fees over 1 %. The math didn't work."

"That sounds backwards," Jenn replied. "Why would anyone keep holding those?"

"Because no one told them they were guaranteed to lose money over certain time periods. Advisors should have also warned people that when interest rates eventually rose, those bond portfolios would get hammered. The smart move would have been to sell the bond funds, lock in gains, and either pay down debt, move the money from bond funds into GICs, or just hold cash until yields reset at better levels."

Lisa blinked. "Even if that meant paying taxes?"

Scott nodded. "Yes. A small tax bill would have been far cheaper than the double-digit losses that followed. When advisors are paid to keep you invested in their products, that needed advice rarely makes it to the table, and you end up being the one who pays for it, sometimes twice. It wasn't complicated. It just needed a little awareness and someone who wasn't afraid to give conflict-free advice."

Jenn muttered, "I think I'm starting to see the game here."

Scott smiled back and leaned forward. "Good, another step towards wealth literacy! Here's how I learned it the hard way."

My Own Wealth Literacy Wake-Up Call

I've always believed in the value of education. But it wasn't until I retired in 2023 that I truly grasped how critical financial literacy is—especially for individuals trying to protect their own wealth. I have two university degrees, a stack of investment industry designations, and I've sat through hundreds of investment presentations, seminars, and conferences over the years. Despite all that training, I can't recall a single session aimed at teaching clients the basic money skills life demands. Financial literacy wasn't on my radar—until it was.

My wake-up call came at a Chartered Professional Accountants (CPA) conference on financial literacy that my partner encouraged me to attend. Sitting in a hotel ballroom in Calgary, I remember thinking, "What could I, a thirty-year industry veteran, possibly learn?" Plenty, as it turned out. I realized most clients never receive even the fundamentals, in part because keeping them in the dark preserves high-cost services.

It was refreshing to see another professional organization champion financial literacy, and sobering to admit my own industry seldom does. Those sessions helped spark this book and clarified a gap. That gap is that financial literacy often fails to give consumers the necessary insight into the *who* and *what* they are dealing with in the financial system. Wealth literacy is intended to fill that gap and level the playing field.

Most banks and financial institutions could do a much better job of educating their clients but too often, they don't. What they do exceptionally well is tighten their grip around the bulk of Canadians' wealth, while charging premium fees. They've also built an oligopolistic and confusing system that leaves too many Canadians anxious and disempowered, as opposed to being optimistic about their financial futures.

Where to Start on Budgeting and Saving

If you're ready to start building your financial literacy, begin with a reliable, unbiased resource. The Financial Consumer Agency of Canada (FCAC) supervises federally regulated financial entities, such as banks and credit unions, and offers objective information on topics like mortgages, credit cards, savings, and practical budgeting tools—a rare place to find guidance without a disguised sales pitch. After that, maybe add a visit or two to your local bookstore or library to deepen your learning. It's time well spent.

Taking Action and Making Your Money Work for You

Ultimately, no one cares about your financial future more than you. Over the years, I've met with hundreds of clients, and one pattern appeared repeatedly. Often, one spouse takes the lead on financial decisions, while the other remains disengaged. That dynamic can seem harmless until the more financially involved partner passes away or is incapacitated, leaving the survivor unaware, unprepared, and overwhelmed.

In my experience, this disconnect isn't about intelligence, capability, or even gender. It is often a simple matter of interest. I've always encouraged the less-engaged spouse to get involved at some level—especially women, who statistically outlive their partners. A better understanding of your financial situation isn't just empowering; it's essential insurance against unexpected change.

Jenn set down her fork. "In our house, I pay the bills and keep track of the accounts. Mike checks in at RRSP season and tax time."

"Guilty." Mike grinned at Jenn. "Maybe I need to finally start paying more attention."

Jenn smiled. “I would like that, dear.”

“And where would Phillip start if he wanted to take his smart brother’s lead?” Pamela asked.

Scott responded, “Imagine *hiring* yourself to run your own financial life. First step is to have an open and curious mindset and realize wealth literacy is the key.”

“Sounds interesting, but what’s the payoff?” Phillip enquired.

“Great question—real dollars, fewer mistakes, and more money working for you. Chances are, it’ll be the highest-paying job you’ve ever had!” Scott declared.

“I’m starting to see how this wealth literacy stuff makes sense, but I think you forgot an important question, Scott,” Phillip replied. “Lisa, is there any more of that awesome cheesecake left?”

CHAPTER 17

Yes, You Need Advice—And a Plan

Lisa smiled at Phillip, "I was hoping you would ask. I made extras. Anyone else want another?" Four hands went up.

Scott waited until the reloaded plates landed. "Tonight, you've learned how to quiet your inner wolves, the biases that can nudge you into costly, emotional moves. While that wins you back control on the inside, we also need to realize that outside pressures, such as market volatility and life changes, do not stop."

Pamela exhaled, "Yes, it's very stressful at times."

Scott nodded, "Agreed, talking helps, but rules and written guidelines specific to our own situation are more useful. We also need to be able to identify when and who we need help from."

Jenn remarked, "So, we need advice from people we trust, and a written plan."

Scott stated. "Exactly. First, decide on what you can control. Next, choose where you'll take the lead and who you'll hire and when. Finally, put it in writing so it lives on paper, not just in your head."

Phillip looked at Pamela and smiled. "Honey, that has brought me to my own hard truth. My do-it-all-myself attitude is not optimal for us. Truth be told, it's stressful and not as easy as I'd thought it would be. I still have a lot to learn; I need more method and less ego."

Pamela nodded her approval, "That's wonderful to hear, Phillip."

Doing-It-Yourself (DIY) Looks Easy— Until It Isn't

"A decade ago, I really did believe that the average investor could do it himself. After all, the flesh was willing, the vehicles were available, and the math wasn't that hard. I was wrong. Having emailed and spoken to thousands of investors over the years, I've come to the sad conclusion that only a tiny minority, at most one percent, are capable of pulling it off."
—William Bernstein, financial author and neurologist

I agree with Dr. Bernstein that only a tiny fraction of people can truly go it alone. That said, I do believe most people can also do much more than they realize or have been led to believe by the financial services industry.

If you review your investment holdings after a nice meal and a couple of glasses of wine following a month or two of strong market performance, or your brother-in-law is crowing about his latest big gains, it can feel easy, and you may wonder why you are paying someone. Please be careful. What looks simple in calm weather can snap under stress.

Most investors lack the experience, perspective, pattern recognition, or other specialized insights seasoned professionals bring. The value of an objective second opinion or an experienced set of eyes only becomes obvious at impact. Markets correct, health changes, jobs shift, and accidents happen. Some lessons arrive the hard way.

The Crash

Jenn smiled, "What lessons are you talking about, Scott?"

"A crash," Scott said. "Not a market crash—but a real one twenty years ago."

Lisa's eyes widened as she spoke softly. "Please tell us."

"It was 10:20 a.m. on December 14, 2005, on one of those rare, bright winter mornings in B.C.'s Lower Mainland with a fresh dusting of snow on the nearby, tree-covered mountains. I was driving along Columbia Street, a familiar route I'd taken thousands of times. Just past downtown New Westminster, I crested the small hill; the traffic light ahead was green."

"BOOM!"

"Oh my God, what happened?" Jenn interjected.

"The oncoming driver missed his curve and hit me head-on. Over the blind crest, I never saw him. I came to in a twisted car, sideways at the curb. A man yelled through the non-existent driver's window. Another opened the passenger door, sniffed, and muttered about smoke. That's when the fear hit—was the car on fire?"

Jenn's grip tightened on her glass. "I can't even imagine that moment."

"Thankfully, it wasn't fire. The *smoke* was powder from six deployed airbags, including the one that saved my eyesight. When I bought the Volvo S60 six months earlier, I'd thought the airbags were an expensive gimmick and even asked about getting a car without them. They weren't a gimmick. The driver's-side curtain airbag had deployed just in time to stop a hail of glass from hitting my face."

"My door was jammed. I was trapped. Emergency crews arrived, covered me with a tarp, and then cut me out with the Jaws of Life. I sat there, immobilized, listening to a local radio station reporting on 'an accident on East Columbia Street,' mine, while glass and car parts crunched underneath passing tires as they prepped me for the short two-minute trip to Royal Columbian Hospital."

"Four hours later, I walked out of the hospital with extremely uneven shoulders, lots of bruising, a few cuts, and wearing what was left of my glasses that had been unceremoniously smashed into my face when the steering wheel airbag had exploded."

Pamela exclaimed, "You're lucky to be alive!"

"You're right, but I felt lucky," Scott said. "Shortly after I reached Trauma Unit 1, another car crash victim was rushed into Unit 2. I lay strapped down, waiting for X-rays, but I could hear the calls to contact his next of kin. I don't know who came to his side, but I still remember his loved ones weeping their goodbyes as he passed away."

Jenn lowered her eyes slowly, "Oh my god, that's terrible."

"Yes, it was." Scott let out a slow breath. "What saved me? A car designed by professionals. Emergency teams trained for the worst. I relied on experts to extract me, assess my condition, and assist me for the long, painful rehab journey that continues to this day. It wasn't one-and-done. It took consistent effort, expert guidance, and a willingness to follow through."

Lisa asked softly, "So, if I understand correctly, you're trying to tell us that even if we want to be do-it-yourself investors, we still need an ongoing plan and professional help every now and then?"

Scott agreed, "Precisely! After thirty years as a portfolio manager, I can take care of my own investments, but there are still aspects of my financial situation that I need guidance on."

(Author's Note: I would like to thank, once again, my friends and family who *nagged* me for years about not wearing my seatbelt. I am sometimes a slow learner, but I am beyond doubt that I would not have authored this book had I not been wearing my seatbelt that day. Given my injuries, I was out of the office for more than a month, but thankfully nobody had to phone the life insurance company that week.)

Your Money Seatbelt

Skill beats intention in a storm. That's why most investors benefit from objective, conflict-free advice and an Investment Policy Statement (IPS). An IPS is a set of rules you draft when you are calm but will follow when you're not. It can be one page or several. Create something suitable for you. It may seem overwhelming at first, so do yourself a favour and hire an investment professional to get it moving. (For a sample IPS, please see the Resource Hub, Chapter 17 at www.scottross.ca.)

Jenn gulped. "I agree we need structure and guardrails, but where do we start?"

Scott began, "Fair enough. Think of your IPS as your money seatbelt and airbags. It will lay out your asset mix, return objectives, time horizon, risk tolerance, future income requirements, and any other investment rules you may want to include. It can also cover taxes and cash needs amongst other things, depending on the level of detail you want. There is no right or wrong, you just need to do it."

"So, a blueprint for our investment process and portfolios?" Mike asked.

Scott nodded, "You got it, but it needs to be in place before you need it, like the airbags in my car. I'll help you, don't worry. Keep in mind, your IPS is separate from your financial plan, but they do need to work in unison."

Jenn confirmed, "Okay, now we've got rules. Who helps with the other aspects of our wealth?"

Scott replied, "We covered it earlier, but here's a quick refresher on when to get advice and who does what."

When to Get Advice

Surviving my crash wasn't about quick thinking—it was about having protection in place before disaster struck. Finances work the same way. When life or markets sideswipe you, you won't have time to research from scratch. You need structure, guidance, and a written plan already in place.

Information Overload: There's a firehose of financial content online, much of it conflicting, some of it misleading, and some flat-out manipulative. A qualified professional can help you filter out the noise.

Changing Life Stages: Your financial needs don't stay the same forever. Buying a home, starting a family, inheriting money, starting a business, getting divorced, retiring, receiving a windfall—each shift creates blind spots. A professional can help you recalibrate your strategy to match your new reality (and avoid getting advice from your cousin Don after his second Christmas eggnog).

Economic and Market Fluctuations: Markets move and economies evolve. Your financial and investment plans can't be a set-it-and-forget-it project. Professional advice helps you adjust to new conditions, avoid panic moves, and spot opportunities that aren't obvious on your newsfeed. Having someone in your corner can mean the difference between a smart move and a costly panic.

Behavioural Biases (a.k.a. Human Brain Problems): We all have psychological biases that can lead us to *doing dumb things* with our money. These may include overspending, excessive borrowing, not saving enough for retirement, or trusting our emotions more than the math. Like a good seatbelt and airbags, a financial professional can counterbalance your worst financial impulses.

Mental Health and Peace of Mind: Money stress is real and can be exhausting. Studies have shown that people who collaborate with a financial advisor often feel more confident, sleep better, and argue less about money with their partners. Don't waste your precious time and mental energy deciphering financial jargon and products or losing sleep over what-ifs. Offload that worry onto someone trained to manage it.

A Refresher on Who Does What

Depending on where you are in your financial journey—building wealth, managing it, or preparing to pass it on—you'll need input from more than one type of professional. Here's a quick refresher on the key players (none of whom are your brother-in-law giving stock tips at Thanksgiving).

Financial Planners and Insurance Advisors: These are your big-picture strategists. They help you with budgeting, retirement planning, insurance needs, and overall goal setting. A solid planner also helps you tie all the moving parts of your financial life together.

Investment Advisors: These are your strategy partners when it comes to building your portfolios. They'll help you choose investments and manage risk, and keep your strategy aligned with your goals. They don't use a crystal ball, nor should you.

Accountants (CPAs): When taxes get tricky, these are your people. They help you reduce tax liability, optimize deductions, plan for major financial moves, and keep your financial records clean. They're not just for tax season, but the money mechanics year-round to keep your financial engine running smoothly. Many can assist you with financial planning as well.

Lawyers and Notaries: When it comes to protecting your legacy, these professionals step in. Wills, powers of attorney, trusts, end-of-life directives and estate transfers are where legal structure matters. Do not DIY legal affairs unless you're hoping to be forever remembered as the reason family Christmas got awkward. I've had more than one lawyer tell me half-jokingly, half-gleefully, that their best clients are the ones who skip legal advice because messy estates mean lots of billable hours.

So, given that advice can be most useful, why don't more people use it?

Why Do People Avoid Advice

We know who does what and when to call them, yet the uncomfortable truth remains that many people still don't hire professional advisors. Some of that hesitation is justified, but avoiding advice altogether can lead to costly mistakes, missed opportunities, and the kind of stress that keeps you up at night. Skepticism is smart, permanent avoidance, not so much. Here are some common objections, and the counters.

"Not sure what advisors do." Ask for a one-page scope with deliverables, hours/year of service and who does the work. No scope, no engagement.

"Bad sales experience." Hire advice-only or fee-for-work professionals with no product compensation.

"Fees feel fuzzy." Demand all-in dollars benchmarked to a low-cost ETF baseline for the same asset mix.

"Privacy worries." Share only what's necessary.

"I can DIY." Great, but start with an IPS and hire hourly for blind spots such as your tax, legal, and estate affairs or more complex reviews.

The bottom line: keep your skepticism, but pair it with process.

Jenn gave a grateful smile. "You're right, Scott. Mike and I do still need guidance. We will start working on our Investment Policy Statement right away. I also want to keep learning so we can eventually do most on our own and stop feeling like we're guessing all the time."

Scott agreed. "That's exactly how it should work, and don't worry, I'll help you get started with your IPS and financial plan. Knowing that the right advice is out there will further empower you and make you a more successful investor."

Phillip chimed in, "So rules first, feelings second."

Scott smiled, "Yes, process and discipline will beat prediction and feelings over time."

Phillip stood up, "Well, gentlemen, speaking of time and seat belts, don't forget the car show tomorrow."

Jenn grinned at Pamela and Lisa, "Hey, while the guys are gone, why don't we plan our annual girls' spa weekend?"

Pamela and Lisa said together, "For sure."

Mike stood. "You coming, Scott?"

Scott laughed and stayed seated, "No, I'm staying for movie night."

"What are you two up to?" Jenn giggled. "And why weren't we invited?"

Lisa blushed, "I asked Scott to watch *The Big Short* with me. It's one of his favourite investment movies, so he offered a play-by-play and a few insights!"

Mike smirked. "Well, that sounds fun, I'm sure he did! Nothing gets the heart racing like subprime mortgage defaults."

Everyone laughed and headed for the door. Mike yelled from the hallway, "Don't forget you're driving us to the car show in the morning!"

Lisa smiled, closing the door slowly, "Thanks for coming, everyone. Good night."

CHAPTER 18

Your Retirement: Designed by You

Scott grabbed his suitcase just as the grey SUV rolled up to the curb. Mike popped the rear hatch, and Scott slid it in with the rest of the luggage already there.

"Hello, ladies … and Mike," Scott grinned as he climbed into the empty front passenger seat.

Jenn leaned forward between the seats, smiling. "It's nice to see you again, Scott. It seems like ages. I'm glad you could come. I like it when Mike and Phillip have a buffer."

Lisa bubbled. "Well, I've seen him plenty." Everyone chuckled.

Lisa glanced at Jenn with a mock scowl. "Hey, I thought this was supposed to be a girls' spa weekend—like last year?"

Mike added, "Phillip and Pamela are meeting us there, so technically it's still half a girls' weekend."

Jenn and Lisa giggled and settled back for the long drive ahead.

The first leg of the drive was full of catching up, minor gossip, and shared stories and movie quotes that sparked mock debates until Jenn leaned her head against the window. "I'm looking forward to retiring. Then we can do this all the time."

"Do what?" Scott asked, deadpan.

"You know," Jenn replied, waving a hand vaguely, "spa weekends, road trips, spontaneous getaways, naps ... basically, not much."

Mike chimed in from behind the wheel. "Don't forget golf. A lot more golf."

Jenn raised an eyebrow. "That's your plan? Golf and not much?"

"Honestly?" Mike responded. "I haven't really thought about it."

At the next red light, Mike glanced over at Scott. "Oh, and by the way, I've hit my full service on the government pension, so I'm retiring in three months."

Lisa sat forward. "Well, we've got a long drive ahead of us. Why don't we talk about what retirement used to mean and what it might mean today?"

Scott agreed. "Perfect. Let's design the life first—then figure out how to fund it."

The Myth of the Golden Age

Before the industrialization of the 19th century, *retirement* wasn't a formal life stage. People worked for as long as they physically could, often until they died. The first modern state pension and retirement age of 65 began in 1880s Germany and is commonly linked to Otto von Bismarck.[43] It was a political tool designed to reduce unemployment and calm unrest, not a moral judgment on when work should end. With average male life expectancy near forty-three at the time, few reached 65, and the pensions cost the state little.

During the 20th century life expectancy in North America increased by approximately 25 years. As people lived longer, the retirement model that many still idealize took root in the post–World War II economic boom as jobs were more stable and employer-sponsored pensions became more common. Retirement, complete with a gold watch and a steady pension, was marketed as the reward for a lifetime of work, a last chapter marked by leisure, comfort, and financial security. It was a powerful image and for a time genuinely achievable.

Today, people live longer, change careers more often, and bear more personal responsibility for their financial futures. Traditional indexed pensions are increasingly rare outside the public sector.

Higher living and healthcare costs, as well as market risks, mean the guaranteed, leisurely retirement is more of a marketing story than reality for most.

Redefining Retirement: A New Chapter, Not the End

Retirement is the freedom to set your own mix of work, leisure, and purpose. It's not stopping, but the option to downshift, reinvent, or re-engage on your terms. Think turns, not a cliff.

Money funds your life, it shouldn't define it, so the better question may be *What does retirement mean to me?* as opposed to *When can I retire?* Draft a blueprint that fits you, not somebody else's checklist. Maybe start with an honest trial run of two to six weeks testing routines, activities, and social rhythms. Then keep what energizes you and cut what doesn't.

Scott shifted in his seat and looked out the window. The silence had stretched just long enough to invite something deeper.

"You know," he sighed, "my retirement didn't start the way I thought it would."

Lisa leaned forward. "Yeah? You never really talked about how it went."

Mike raised an eyebrow. "But you had a plan, right? You didn't just walk out on Friday and disappear."

"That was the idea," Scott said with a small shrug. "I had my finances sorted out and had had enough of the corporate schtick; it really didn't resonate anymore. The whole checklist was there: a little travel, a lot of golf, start a hobby or two. But once I stepped away, it fell flat."

Jenn leaned forward. "What do you mean?"

Scott continued, "I had time, I had freedom, but little direction. The structure I thought I hated was what had kept me grounded. Without it, I was just floating, doing more of nothing, dabbling in a few things that didn't stick, and sometimes wondering what the point of it was."

Lisa nodded. "You didn't expect to feel lost."

"Nope. I expected freedom, but instead, I felt disconnected. Some days, I didn't really have a reason to get out of bed, which threw me for a loop. Other days, I felt like I didn't belong anywhere." Scott paused. "That feeling, it can creep up fast when no one's asking anything of you."

Mike looked over. "So, what did you do?"

"Eventually, I started rebuilding. A little structure, a little purpose. I said yes to some volunteer work. Started writing, too. Not because I had to, but because I needed something to focus on. Something that felt like mine."

Jenn smiled. "I guess that's the part no one tells you—retirement isn't a vacation. It's what comes after the vacation ends."

Scott nodded. "Yes. I didn't retire to do nothing. I just didn't know what I was retiring into. Took me a while to figure it out. And another observation, every version of retirement rests on two pillars."

Health and Wealth: The Twin Pillars in Your Retirement

Retirement planning often centers around money, but financial freedom is only one side of the equation. The other side is health.

You can have all the money you need, but if your physical or mental health deteriorates, the freedom you worked for shrinks. Likewise, great health without a financial foundation can lead to stress, instability, and hard choices down the line. They reinforce each other, and both need attention.

Health is the engine that powers your lifestyle. It determines what you can do, where you go, what you enjoy, and how independent you remain. Regular activity, good nutrition, preventive care, and strong social connections can all impact your quality of life and how long your options stay open. Start early, as habits compound. No amount of money can buy back mobility, energy, or peace of mind.

Wealth will give you options for housing, healthcare, and new pursuits, so you can live on your terms.

Balance is the goal, not perfection. You don't want to outlive your money or your mobility. Design for both and thrive.

Building Your Financial Foundation

Retirement runs on a solid, flexible financial structure that can support your lifestyle, absorb surprises, and adapt over time. That starts with understanding your full financial picture and preparing for what is likely, what is possible, and knowing what is out of your control.

Know where you stand with the basics, including your net worth, your income sources, and how your assets align with your liabilities and liquidity. Retirement is not just about what you have, it is also about how easily you can access it and how long it will last.

Your sources of retirement income might include employer pensions, government benefits, personal savings and investments or other income streams such as real estate, royalties, small business earnings, or part-time work.

For workers who contributed, income will also include Canada Pension Plan (CPP) benefits. While age 65 is the standard age to start your CPP, you can start any time from age 60 to 70 years of age. Your payments will be reduced if taken before age 65 and increased if deferred until after age 65. CPP is paid monthly for life and indexed to inflation.

Old Age Security (OAS) is also payable at 65, and deferrable to 70, provided you meet residency requirements. For higher-income Canadians, some or all their OAS may be clawed back. Some individuals may also qualify for the Guaranteed Income Supplement (GIS), an income-tested top-up based on their income and marital status.

Outside the public sector, where defined-benefit (DB) plans are most common, most workplace arrangements are defined-contribution (DC) plans or group RRSPs. You should include RRSPs/RRIFs, TFSAs, and non-registered accounts in your income sources map.

Reality Check: You might not be as liquid or secure as you think. Home equity should not be considered *cash* as you need a place to live, and overly optimistic investment return assumptions can paint an overly rosy picture. Please keep in mind that financial planners and investment advisors can be prone to telling people *what they want to hear* as opposed to what they need to hear. They may offer overly hopeful return projections or hesitate to be fully transparent about your situation, fearing it would upset you and risk losing your account. Ask for plain-language numbers and written assumptions.

Once you have the numbers, the next question is simple: "How much can I safely withdraw from my portfolio each year without running out of money?"

Sustainability and Withdrawal Strategies

This is where the well-known *4% Rule* steps in. It states that you can begin making withdrawals of approximately 4% of your portfolio value, then increase that amount each year by the rate of inflation. For example, if you had $100,000 invested, you could withdraw $4,000 in year one. If inflation was three percent in year one, you would then withdraw $4,120 in year 2 ($4,000 + $120 (3% X $4,000)), and so on.

The 4% rule is a useful baseline, but it is far from bulletproof. Based on when you start withdrawing your money, market volatility, interest rate changes, inflation, and unexpected life events, you may need to adjust your sustainable withdrawal rate. It's always best to err on the conservative side. If you're too conservative, you can always give yourself a raise later. If you're too aggressive, you risk experiencing *money death*, which is when you run out of money before you take your last breath. Here is a practical *guardrails* approach:

Set your target rate and guardrail percentages. For example, target a 4% withdrawal rate with a lower guardrail at 3% and an upper guardrail at 5%.

After strong return years in the market, allow a real or above-inflation raise of 3% to 5% if your effective withdrawal rate falls below your lower guardrail of 3%.

After poor return years, trim next year's real spending by 5% to 10% if your effective withdrawal rate rises above your upper guardrail of 5%, or you risk your portfolio declining meaningfully.

Seek advice from an investment professional if you are not sure what is appropriate for your situation.

Building a strong financial base won't predict the future, but it will prepare you for it. Common lifestyle, health, or financial disruptors can strike at any time. These can include changes in energy levels, long-term care needs, family obligations or government benefit changes, amongst others. Keep a small cash or short-term bond buffer on hand for both your peace of mind and to avoid selling in down markets. To further protect yourself, examine your insurance needs and keep coverages current. These could include life, health/dental, critical-illness, long-term care and disability.

The conversation had drifted into a comfortable lull as the scenery shifted from highway to rolling countryside.

Jenn broke the cadence. "So, has anyone here ever written down their retirement plan?"

Mike joked. "Define *written*. I've got a government pension, a golf membership, and a credit card. Does that count?"

Lisa replied. "I have a list somewhere. It's mostly travel ideas, wineries I want to visit, and a half-baked idea for a dog rescue."

Scott joked, "That's better than my first retirement plan." The whole car laughed. "It doesn't have to be perfect, just intentional." He added, "Take the time to figure out what matters to you, make a rough sketch, and give yourself room to adapt. Be honest with the numbers and yourself; you are the one who must live with your plan."

"And leave room for surprises," Lisa remarked. "Because they're coming one way or another."

Mike interjected, "Speaking of surprises, those are some nasty-looking clouds rolling our way. I'm glad we're going to get there before that storm hits."

Lisa pointed out the window, "There it is—Collingwood. Eighteen kilometres!" The mood in the car lifted instantly. Jenn and Lisa exchanged excited glances.

"I can already smell eucalyptus and overpriced cucumber water," Jenn said, beaming.

"You think they'll have those hot stones again?" Lisa gushed.

As the SUV picked up speed toward the spa, the conversation turned to dinner reservations, massage preferences, and whether Scott could be trusted with the wine list.

CHAPTER 19

Lessons Learned: The Keys to Your Financial Success

The next morning, Jenn opened her eyes slowly, feeling more rested than she had in weeks. Mike was already up, lounging in a chair, scrolling through his phone. The alarm clock on the nightstand was blinking.

"Looks like the power went out last night," she mumbled, stretching.

"Yeah," Mike said without looking up. "Storm must have knocked something out. I just got a text from Phillip. He and Pamela made it in. They'll join us later for breakfast."

Jenn sat up, brushing her hair back. "Are they okay?"

"Yeah. They got stuck behind a downed tree, but they're here."

She nodded, already thinking about breakfast. "Let's go find the others. I need coffee before anyone tries to talk to me about investments or taxes."

Downstairs, low voices threaded through the dining room, and the air smelled of coffee and warm muffins. Lisa and Scott were already seated.

"Morning, guys," Jenn said, sliding into a chair. "We heard from Phillip and Pamela. They'll be down soon. They arrived late last night because of the storm."

A staff member appeared with a tray of small glasses. "Spa appointments have been delayed," she announced. "Some of our staff are still making their way in. In the meantime, mimosas are complimentary."

"Mimosas and time," Jenn said, settling in. "Might as well pick up where we left off last night."

Scott turned toward her. "Actually, Jenn, I've been meaning to say I'm really impressed. You've come a long way. Your planning, your confidence, your wealth literacy. It's not always easy stuff."

Jenn winked. "Thanks. I've had some good guidance. Here's the thing I keep asking myself. Can you really *succeed* financially just by doing the right things? Or is a lot of it just luck?"

Scott paused. "Luck is always a factor, but most outcomes are behaviour driven, and fortunately, that's the part you can control."

The elevator chimed and the doors slid open. Phillip and Pamela stepped into the dining room.

"We made it," Phillip exclaimed. "There was a tree down on Concession 5 road, but we're here."

Pamela smiled. "And absolutely ready for breakfast."

"Perfect timing," Scott replied, waving them over. "Grab a seat. We were just getting into the good part."

Jenn glanced around the table. "Why don't we list it out. Not the usual technical stuff—just the mindsets and habits that make a difference."

Secrets of Success: The Mindsets That Matter

Financial success isn't just about picking the right investments or following the latest economic forecasts. The greatest investors—the most consistent, resilient, and satisfied—share a handful of mindsets and habits that have little to do with market predictions and everything to do with personal behaviour. The good news is that all these traits are available to you.

You Focus on What You Can Control. Markets are unpredictable. So are interest rates, inflation, and geopolitical events. Focus your energy on the parts of your plan you can influence, like fees, taxes, asset allocation, savings rate, and your own behaviour. This mindset reduces stress, sharpens clarity and puts you back in the driver's seat. You may not control the road, but you do control the wheel.

You Make an Effort. You don't passively drift through decisions, you stay engaged, keep learning, and ask questions. You don't have to master every detail, but you do need to understand the basics, enough to avoid the worst mistakes and recognize when advice is biased or off base. Curiosity pays compound interest in this world.

You Are Patient and Disciplined. You know the biggest gains often come from sticking to a plan and not chasing the newest trend or reacting to headlines. You trust time over timing and understand that wealth is built gradually, not dramatically.

You Avoid Emotional Traps. You don't try to outrun fear or ride waves of excitement, and you understand that panic and greed are terrible decision-makers. Instead, you revisit your goals and make changes only when needed, guided by research and reason, not reaction.

You Practice Humility. Don't try to outsmart the market. Respect the fact that markets are powered by collective intelligence and that overconfidence is often the first step to your underperformance. Staying humble may be the most underrated wealth strategy, especially when things are going well. You need to avoid shortcuts, stay grounded, and stick to strategies you understand.

You Have Clear, Written Goals. You don't invest aimlessly but toward something like retirement at a certain age, funding a child's education, or simply maintaining freedom of choice. Goals provide structure and help you cut through noise and distraction.

You Know Yourself. Self-awareness is key. You understand your tolerance for risk, your emotional triggers, and the timeframes that work for you. Don't copy someone else's design, but build one that matches your actual life.

You Reassess Without Overreacting. Check in periodically, not obsessively. You review your progress, adjust as needed, and revisit your goals when life changes. You don't overcorrect with every market dip and trust your long-term plan more than short-term noise.

You Keep It Simple. Avoid unnecessary complexity. The more complicated a product is, the higher the likely costs and the lower the odds you outperform after fees. If you can't explain it to a friend in under two minutes, it's probably too complicated.

The above aren't techniques but disciplines. They form the foundation for every financial decision and are the filter that removes short-term noise in favour of long-term wisdom. Markets will always change, your behaviours shouldn't.

Pamela reached for her second coffee. "So … mindset is the foundation."

"Exactly," Scott said. "But even the best mindset won't save a sloppy plan."

Lisa raised her mimosa glass. "And here's to not learning things the hard way."

Mike smirked. "Too late. I've got lifetime status on the hard way."

Everyone laughed, not because it was funny, but because it was true. They'd all made mistakes, but they were also learning, and the next phase was about doing better with what they knew.

Blueprint Before Buying

Smart planning doesn't have to be complicated, but it must be intentional. Here are some of the most valuable and often overlooked lessons that tend to surface after something has gone sideways.

A Great Portfolio Won't Fix a Bad Plan. It's easy to obsess over returns and performance metrics, but they don't mean much if they're not aligned with your real-life goals. Planning isn't just about numbers. It's also about integrating your investments with your tax situation, estate needs, retirement vision, and personal values.

Live Within Your Means (For Real). This principle is timeless for a reason. Overspending, even just slightly, erodes savings faster than most people realize. The most common financial trap isn't market losses or bad investments but lifestyle creep. Live within your means and resist the urge to constantly upgrade. The Dickens line still applies: "Annual income twenty pounds, annual expenditure nineteen six, result happiness."

Get Your Legal House in Order. Wills, powers of attorney, beneficiary designations, none of it is glamorous, but all of it is essential. People often delay these steps because they feel uncomfortable or overwhelmed. However, when something unexpected happens, these are the documents that protect you and your family from confusion, conflict, and unnecessary costs. You aren't finished until the legal pieces are in place.

Pay for Value, Not Just Assets. Not all advice is created equal, and neither is its cost. One hard-earned lesson is that many advisors are paid for what you have, not for what you need. Always understand how your financial professionals are compensated, and whether their incentives align with your goals. A glossy brochure isn't valuable; clarity, trust and transparency are.

Your Financial Plan ≠ Your Investment Plan. It's broader, deeper, and more personal. Investments are just one tool. The planning process is the framework that gives those tools direction and purpose.

Jenn set down her mug. "So, the foundation goes in first?"

Scott nodded. "Yes. Planning isn't optional. It's the blueprint that makes everything else work. The next challenge is what to do with your money."

Lisa grinned. "Translation: stop shopping for products, start following a process."

Mike chuckled. "And no more 'I saw a headline investing.'"

Phillip raised a brow. "Or neighbour-with-a-hot-tip investing."

Pamela rolled her eyes at Phillip and then leaned in. "Okay then—where does it all go?"

Scott said, "Into a portfolio that matches your risk tolerance, time horizon, and minimizes your tax load. Next stop, investment lessons learned."

Process Over Prediction

If planning is where people fail quietly, investing is where they fail loudly. It shows up as chasing hot tips, making predictions, overcomplicating strategies, and checking a portfolio like a defibrillator. Smart investing isn't about outperforming others in the short term; it's about avoiding your own worst instincts. Most of these lessons get learned the hard way—after a market drop, a slick product pitch, or a gut call that didn't age well.

There's No One *Right* Strategy. Everyone wants a perfect formula, but the best investment strategy is the one you'll stick with, especially when things get volatile. Your personal timeline, risk tolerance, and temperament matter more than what's trending on financial podcasts.

Simplicity Wins, Complexity Taxes. Complexity usually adds three costs: higher fees, more taxes and more behavioural mistakes. Own a portfolio you know, it's what helps you stay calm when things get weird.

Passive Isn't Passive. Index funds are popular for a reason, but don't assume they're foolproof. Every *passive* portfolio still involves decisions: which index to use, how to rebalance, and what to exclude. Passive investing is a great tool, but it's not a set-it-and-forget-it machine.

Wealth ≠ Skill. Having money doesn't prove you have investing skill, and *exclusive* access often just means higher fees. Smart investing is about fit and discipline, not access.

Don't Watch It Every Day. Constant portfolio-checking doesn't make you more informed. It just makes you more emotional. Data shows we feel losses two to three times more intensely than gains. Watching every dip trains your brain to panic. Step back. Check in periodically and protect your emotional capital.

Mike chuckled and held up his phone. "Permission to delete this 'FOMO Stock Alert' app from my home screen?"

Jenn smiled. "Granted—quarterly checkups, not daily drama."

Scott stated, "Exactly. The antidote to drama is simple: process over prediction. Here are a few rules for when your money hits your account."

Trade the Crystal Ball for a process.

Invest With a Process, not a Prediction. Good investing means having a repeatable process and sticking to it. When you invest based on emotion, timing, or gut instinct, you're not managing money, you're gambling.

Diversify, Don't De-Worsify. Diversification is real, but it's not just about owning lots of stuff. Too much overlap turns a portfolio into a cluttered mess that simply mimics the market with extra fees. Own enough to spread risk but not so much that you lose the plot.

Investments Don't Care Who Owns Them. Your investments don't know you. They don't care how hard you worked for your money, how confident you feel, or how many spreadsheets you made. They do reward fit with your plan, risk management, and time.

Use Your TFSAs Strategically, Not Recklessly. Tax-free savings accounts (TFSAs) are powerful but only when used wisely. They're a place for structured, long-term growth, and the long-term tax-free compounding they provide is your greatest ally over time. Don't treat it like a casino account.

This Time is Different. No four words have consistently cost investors more money through history than that single flawed belief. If you hear these words, pause, and then check your process.

Phillip swirled the last of his mimosa. "I still honestly think that stock was different. Supposed insider tip from the neighbour, new tech, early buzz, right place, right time."

"Let me guess," Jenn grinned. "You also told yourself this time was different?"

He pointed at her with his spoon and replied, "Those exact words."

Mike leaned back. "Classic, brother. The most expensive phrase in investing."

Scott remarked, "Markets love it when we think we've outsmarted them. That's when they bite back."

Jenn stated, "Alright. Let's talk about markets, the final frontier."

The Market Doesn't Care

The market is indifferent and doesn't know you. It doesn't care about you or your retirement goals, and it doesn't reward good behaviour or punish bad luck. It moves on sentiment, data, noise, and billions of decisions you'll never see. What you believe about the market will be tested; what you assume will be corrected; and what you ignore may be what costs you.

Risk and Return Travel Together. The promise of higher returns always comes with more risk because there is no shortcut around it. If something looks too good to be true, it probably is. Investors often get burned chasing upside while pretending downside doesn't exist. Please remember, you can't separate the two.

Markets Don't Always Make Sense. Over extended periods, prices tend to reflect fundamentals and be rational. The trouble is the stretch between now and then. In the short term, market movements can be driven by valuations, money flows, headlines, algorithms, and investor emotions that can all swing prices in ways that defy explanation.

Time in the Market Beats *Timing the Market.* Trying to guess when to get in or out of the market almost always does more harm than good. If you miss just a handful of the best days it can erase years of your gains. Long-term compounding wins, timing rarely does.

Markets Are Forward-Looking. Economic news doesn't move markets the way most people expect. That's because the market is already trying to price in what's coming next, not what is happening today. When the news breaks, the market may have already moved. Trying to trade headlines is like trying to win a race that started before you got to the track.

Most Funds Don't Beat the Market. It's hard to consistently outperform the market, especially after fees. Most actively managed funds underdeliver despite their glossy brochures. Low-cost, diversified strategies often quietly outperform the hype, and chasing performance is a game most investors lose.

Markets are unpredictable, messy, and indifferent, but they're not impossible. You don't have to control them; you just have to understand how they behave and the fact that you can't predict them in the short to medium term. Also, understand how you will behave when they misbehave. Stay humble, stay invested and stop pretending you're the one in charge.

Jenn asked, "So, financial success is a behaviour system, not about reacting to market noise?"

Scott replied, "Yes, if you have a solid process that creates discipline, that discipline will create positive outcomes for you."

Just then, the server returned, balancing a tray of empty glasses and with good news. "Ladies, the spa is back up and running. In fact, we're a few minutes ahead of schedule."

"Yes!" Lisa shouted, throwing both hands in the air.

Jenn turned towards the guys. "What are you three doing while we soak our way to enlightenment?"

Mike smiled. "Well, since it's warmed up a few degrees and the roads are clear, we're heading down to the Canadian Golf Museum."

Pamela glanced at Jenn and Lisa, then smiled at the men. "Have fun, gentlemen. We'll see you at dinner—after our spa day and several hours of not talking about markets."

CHAPTER 20

It's Your Money: What's Your Next Move?

Steam

Steam was supposed to be relaxing. Jenn had followed the others in with good intentions and a fluffy white towel, cinched a touch too tightly, as if it could somehow pin her nerves in place. It didn't.

As the mist thickened around her, so did the pressure in her chest. The warmth wasn't comforting; it was suffocating. She tried to breathe through it, but all she could think about was the decision she'd been dragging around for weeks.

"Stay with the new advisor … or own it."

Heat flushed her skin, her stomach tightened further. "I need some air," Jenn blurted. She stood and reached for the steam room door.

Lisa's head snapped up in concern. "Jenn? You, okay?"

"Yeah," she lied, grabbing her water bottle. "Just hot."

Air

Outside, she lay on a wooden bench beside the infinity pool. She hated how unsure she still felt, and how every pro and con she'd listed, and relisted, kept looping in her head. Yet as the nausea ebbed, something else surfaced—a flicker of clarity. A tiny, stubborn voice whispered, "You already know what to do."

The Decision Lands

Lisa and Pamela, each carrying a glass of cucumber water, found Jenn a little later.

Pamela smiled, "You're looking much better now."

"Thanks, I am feeling better," Jenn replied. "I can't wait for our hot stone massages."

Soon, Jenn was on the massage table, face down, hands unclenched, forehead in the cradle. The therapist kneaded warm citrus oil into her back, her breath slowed, the noise receded. Her mind cleared. She thought of the simple rules they'd written down: plan first, keep fees low, automate the boring parts, and use guardrails when markets get loud. She didn't need permission—just a start date. By her third exhale, as the therapist traced a calm line across her shoulder blades, she understood. This wasn't a leap; it was the next step.

"No more fence-sitting. I'll manage our finances, and seek advice when we need it, on our terms."

The Room

Later in her room, still warm from the massage, Jenn dressed slowly, but intentionally. She now felt lighter and looser, not so much in her body as in her mind. Her choice was made.

Mike poked his head in, just back from the golf museum. "Hey, dear, how was your spa day?"

"Amazing. I think I melted in there." Jenn turned and added with a slow grin. "I made my decision."

Mike straightened, and his smile turned to concern. "Oh ... what decision?"

Jenn beamed at her husband. "I'm taking it over. Our money, our decisions. It's ours now."

Mike looked at Jenn like she'd just told him she'd won the lottery. "I've been waiting for you to pull the trigger on that. You've been chewing on it for weeks."

She nodded. "Yeah. It finally clicked. I feel ... free."

"Then let's toast to that," Mike said, offering his arm like the drama queen he occasionally was.

The Toast

By the time everyone sat down at the table draped in white linen, the faint scent of garlic butter drifting in the air, Jenn was brimming with quiet excitement. She didn't want to make a speech, but the words pressed behind her smile.

She tapped her glass gently with the back of her fork. Heads turned. "I'll keep this short," she shared.

"Today, I made a big decision. I'm taking control of our finances. I've got the tools now. I just needed the guts."

She looked at Lisa, then Mike. "Thank you both for standing alongside me through this."

Lisa smiled, eyes misting. "That's awesome, sis."

Jenn turned to Scott. "Thank you for being our guide and letting me ask every *dumb* question. Your patience, honesty, and clarity allowed me to see behind the curtain and provided the confidence to finally take control of our family's wealth."

Ownership Tastes Better.

Scott raised his glass. "Proud of you. There are no dumb questions and I'm here if you want a second set of eyes."

Lisa chimed in, "Hear, hear."

Glasses clinked and the night unfurled around them—warm, open, and free of spreadsheets.

It's Your Move

If you have ever felt even a flicker of what Jenn did, do not file it—act. You can start here.

Within 72 Hours

- Write a one-page Money Pledge (goals, target asset mix, risk ranges, re-balance bands).
- List every account and calculate your all-in costs.

Over the Next 90 Days

- Book an advice-only consult for specific questions—on your terms.
- Consolidate stray accounts; simplify overlapping funds.
- Create your Investment Policy Statement and rebalance your portfolio, if needed.
- Create Decision Rules for turbulence (rebalance thresholds; no impulse buys).

Commitment: "I will make my first move by MM/DD and review progress in 90 days."

CHAPTER 21

The Road Ahead: Own Your Financial Tomorrow

Scott whispered in Lisa's ear, "Good morning, sunshine," and kissed her forehead.

"Morning," she murmured, still half-asleep.

Scott grinned, "You've had that adorable smile on your face for the past half hour. You look so happy."

"I had the loveliest vision," Lisa replied dreamily. "It was about Jenn, a year from now. She had become the empowered investor you've been talking about—confident, calm, in control. She kept day-to-day money at her favourite bank but moved their investments to the bank's discount brokerage, saving thousands per year. You helped her at first, then connected her with someone else to step in."

Scott laughed. "I thought I was retired. Now I'm working in your dream?"

"That one decision allowed her to semi-retire four years early," Lisa smiled. "More time with Mike and the kids. She even volunteers at the animal shelter and helps with the historical society fundraiser. Our parents would be thrilled."

Scott squeezed her hand. "Great dream. Make sure you tell her!"

Scott checked the time. "Hey, we'd better get rolling. We don't want to keep the others waiting for breakfast, and you have your spa appointment."

A short while later, they joined the others in the dining room. Spotting her sister, Lisa rushed forward, arms open. "Good morning, Jenn! I had the most remarkable dream about your future self!"

"Well, good morning to you, too! I hope it was a good one!" Jenn grinned, intrigued.

Lisa's smile widened. "You'll love it! I'll tell you all about it at the spa this morning! Also, Scott has news."

After everyone was seated, Scott set his cup down. "Jenn, you nudged me to write the book I kept dodging. It's now real."

He glanced around the table. "You all asked the tough questions, and I realized something simple: People's needs should outrank industry habits. I'm putting the wolves' playbook in Canadians' hands so they can act in their own best interests. It'll be plain English, real math, no sales pitches."

Scott looked at Lisa. "And this woman backed me even when I thought it might end up as a 400-page keepsake for my kids. Thank you, Lisa."

Lisa leaned in, eyes warm. "You're welcome."

Everyone broke into smiles. Jenn squeezed Scott's arm. "Good."

Mike deadpanned, "So you're finally writing it down for the rest of us?" Laughter circled the table.

They ordered, ate, traded a few more jokes, and the women headed for the spa.

Becoming the Architect of Your Financial Future

"The best way to predict the future is to create it."
—Peter Drucker

There is no magical shortcut to becoming an empowered investor. The shift from confusion to clarity, and from anxiety to confidence, comes from transforming knowledge into deliberate, actionable steps. Here's what a richer life looks like.

The Empowered Investor:

- Controls what they can (costs, structure, behaviour) and accepts what they can't control.
- Thinks in processes, not predictions.
- Stays curious and invests time in learning.
- Believes that wealth literacy brings freedom, not just facts.
- Builds confidence, lowers stress, and owns their decisions.
- Grows and protects wealth with purpose for family, future and giving back.
- Welcomes guidance but never hands over the wheel.
- Automates discipline with scheduled rebalancing and reviews.
- Writes out a plan and an IPS with rules and guidelines.
- Chooses advisors who are objective, trustworthy, and jargon-free.

After the spa, everybody met back at the resort restaurant for lunch. Scott, Mike, and Phillip were at a corner table, half-watching the Golf Channel.

Jenn called as they walked into the restaurant, "Hey, everyone."

Phillip smiled. "You all look radiant this afternoon!"

"It was an awesome morning. We should come here again," Jenn said, beaming. She was still glowing from her facial and from yesterday's decision to take charge.

Jenn looked over at Scott. "Even though I've decided to take control of our financial future, I have been thinking about the playing field other Canadians face. Can you share a few thoughts on how you see it, and what could make it better for all of us?"

Scott grinned, "Thanks for asking. Why don't we order, and I'll share a few thoughts."

A More Prosperous, Confident Canada

Societal Benefits. When investors hold the financial services industry to account, households get steadier. Saving, spending, and investing increase, stimulating economic growth. That confidence also helps shrink wealth gaps by bringing in groups such as first-time investors, new graduates, and underrepresented communities. The result is a more inclusive system that fuels upward mobility, stronger communities, and better-funded public services that include healthcare, education, and infrastructure.

Enhancing Innovation and Opportunity. Trust unlocks capital. When people know their money is managed transparently, they will back local businesses, startups and emerging technologies. That flow of capital also sparks new ideas, creates higher-quality, higher-paying jobs, and positions Canada as a hub for entrepreneurship—a key driver of long-term prosperity and wealth creation.

Stronger Communities and Infrastructure. Greater household financial security yields more resilient government revenues from taxes and consumer spending. This stability enhances Canada's reputation for quality of life and creates a virtuous circle. Stability fuels growth and growth reinforces stability.

A Destination for Investment. Less red tape, greater transparency, and respect for the free market won't just help families; they will make Canada a magnet for capital and talent. The outcome: more investment, better jobs, and a stronger foundation for long-term resilience.

A Global Leader in Ethical Finance. By marrying plain-language disclosure, fiduciary duty, and education, Canada can set the gold standard for an integrity-driven financial system, but it starts with each of us.

Reasonable, Transparent, Plain-Language Fees. A clear, plain-language one-page fee disclosure should be standard. It would list investment management fees, advice and planning costs, trading fees, any other expenses, and would show an equivalent hourly rate for services provided.

A Profession That Puts You First. The financial services industry has reinvented itself before; now it must do so for consumers. The foundations already exist in bodies like the CFA Institute and FP Canada, but what's missing is a national commitment to consistent, enforced standards so advice is truly client-first. Raise the bar with higher entry and conduct standards, a unified licensing framework, and an enforceable code of ethics—more like medicine or law.

Closing Note

From Jenn's all-too-real nightmare to Lisa's hopeful dream, one truth stands out: your future is largely built by you. Demand better and help build it. If enough Canadians do the same, we won't just improve our own balance sheets; we'll shape a financial system that's transparent, ethical, and prosperous for all.

The group lingered over empty coffee cups as the waiter dropped off the cheques.

"Scott," Pamela said, "as the membership director at the Small Business Association, I'd love you to share these insights with our members. They really need this kind of straight talk."

Scott smiled. "I'm technically retired, but helping people uncover hidden fees and levelling the playing field with their bank beats working on my golf game. Let me think it over, and we'll chat next week."

The table erupted in nods and good-natured teasing. Plans were made to turn the getaway into an annual tradition—same lodge, even more laughs.

As they piled into the SUV, Scott finished loading the bags. He got into the back seat beside Lisa, leaned forward, and grinned at Jenn. “Buckle up, Jenn. You’re in the driver’s seat now.”

Common Titles Of Professionals Who Assist With Your Finances

CFA Chartered Financial Analyst: Institutional-level investment research, portfolio building, and ethics expertise.

CFP Certified Financial Planner: Comprehensive planning, retirement, cash flow, taxes, insurance, investments, estate basics.

CIM Chartered Investment Manager: Canadian designation for portfolio construction, analysis, and discretionary management.

CIWM Certified International Wealth Manager: Advanced private-wealth management across investments, tax, and estate planning.

CLU Chartered Life Underwriter: Advanced insurance, estate transfer, and business succession planning.

CPA Chartered Professional Accountant: Tax preparation, planning, compliance, and corporate accounting.

FCSI Fellow of Canadian Securities Institute: Senior fellowship recognizing experience and education.

LLB Lawyer: Prepares legal documents and provides advice on wills, estates, real estate, and business matters.

NP Notary/Notary Public: Handle wills and real-estate contracts.

PFA Professional Financial Advisor : Advocis designation focused on advice delivery and client-care standards.

PFP Personal Financial Planner: Planning designation emphasizing personal finance and foundational advice.

PM Portfolio Manager: A financial professional who makes investment decisions and manages investment portfolios for individuals or institutions.

RFP Registered Financial Planner: Holistic planning designation emphasizing ethics and plan quality.

RRC Registered Retirement Consultant: Retirement income, taxation, and withdrawal-strategy planning.

Glossary

10-Year Government of Canada Bond. Benchmark bond often used to gauge interest-rate levels and risk-free returns in Canada.

60/40 Portfolio. A common mix of 60% stocks and 40% bonds used for balanced investing.

Absolute Return. The total return of an investment without comparing it to a benchmark.

Active Management. Trying to beat the market by selecting securities or timing trades.

Active Share. Percentage of a fund's holdings that differ from its benchmark.

Adjusted Cost Base (ACB). Your tax cost for a security, used to calculate capital gains/losses.

After-Tax Return. What you keep after taxes on interest, dividends, and capital gains income.

Alpha. Return above what risk alone would predict; the manager's value-add.

Alternative Investments. Assets beyond stocks/bonds such as hedge funds and real estate.

Annualized Return. Average compound return per year over a multi-year period.

Annuity. Product that converts capital into guaranteed income.

Asset Allocation. How you split money among stocks, bonds, cash, and alternatives.

Assets Under Administration (AUA). Client assets a firm administers.

Assets Under Management (AUM). Client assets a firm manages, often with discretion.

Baseline or Reference Portfolio. A baseline is the lowest-cost, broadly diversified portfolio that already fits your goals and risk. It is the control you price everything against.

Basis Point (bps). One one-hundredth of a percent (0.01%).

Behaviour Gap. Difference between a fund's return and what its investors actually earn due to poor investor behaviour.

Benchmark. A standard reference index (e.g., S&P 500) used to compare performance.

Beta. Sensitivity of a security/portfolio to market movements.

Bid-Ask Spread. The gap between what buyers pay and sellers receive, a hidden trading cost.

Canada Deposit Insurance Corporation (CDIC). Federal deposit insurer for eligible deposits at member institutions (limits apply).

Canadian Investor Protection Fund (CIPF). Protects client property if a CIRO dealer becomes insolvent (not market losses).

Canadian Investment Regulatory Organization (CIRO). National Self-Regulatory Organization for investment/mutual fund dealers and marketplaces.

Canadian Securities Administrators (CSA). Council coordinating provincial/territorial securities regulators.

Capital Gain/Loss. Profit or loss when you sell an investment for more/less than ACB.

Capital Gains Inclusion Rate. Portion of realized gains that is taxable in Canada (rate subject to change).

Carbon Dioxide (CO2). Major greenhouse gas; baseline unit for emissions accounting and targets.

Cash Buffer. Cash set aside to fund near-term spending and avoid selling investments in a downturn.

Cash Drag. Lower return from holding excess cash instead of invested assets.

Churning. Excessive trading that advisors conduct to increase compensation without client benefit.

Client Focused Reforms (CFR). Canadian rules requiring advisors to put client interests first in key areas.

Client Relationship Model Phase 2 (CRM2). Rules requiring clearer cost and performance reporting to clients.

Closet Indexing. An active fund that hugs its benchmark but charges active fees.

Compound Interest. Earned interest on interest; the engine of long-term growth.

Correlation. How closely two assets move together; low correlation helps diversification.

Cost of Advice. What you pay all-in (fees, commissions, embedded costs) for advisory services.

Credit Rating. An agency's opinion of an issuer's creditworthiness (e.g., AAA to junk).

Credit Risk. Risk of loss if a borrower cannot meet obligations.

Current Yield. A bond's annual coupon divided by its current market price.

Custodian. Firm that safeguards client assets and settles trades.

Deferred Sales Charge (DSC) or Back-End Load. A redemption fee if a mutual fund is sold before a scheduled date, typically 6 years after the purchase date (a.k.a. Didn't See that Coming.)

Defined Benefit Pension (DB Pension). Employer plan paying a formula-based lifetime income.

Defined Contribution Pension (DC Pension). Employer plan where contributions are defined and retirement income depends on returns.

Discount Brokerage. Firm offering low-cost self-directed trading with limited advice.

Discretion. Written authority allowing a portfolio manager to place trades in your account without obtaining approval but within the goals, asset mix, and risk limits you've agreed to in writing.

Diversification. Spreading investments across assets to reduce the risk of a single failure.

Dividend. A cash distribution from a company's profits (not guaranteed).

Embedded Commission. Fees built into product pricing (e.g., trailer fees in mutual funds).

Environmental, Social, Governance (ESG). A set of metrics used to evaluate a company beyond its financial performance.

Equity. Ownership in a company (common stock).

Exchange-Traded Fund (ETF). Pooled fund trading on an exchange, generally low-cost and tax-efficient.

Financial Consumer Agency of Canada (FCAC). Federal agency overseeing consumer protection in financial services.

Financial Literacy. Practical understanding of money, investing, borrowing, and planning.

Financial Transactions and Reports Analysis Centre of Canada (FINTRAC). Federal anti-money-laundering/terrorist-financing oversight agency.

Fixed Income. Bonds and similar securities that pay interest.

Fund Facts / ETF Facts. Disclosure documents summarizing costs, risks, performance.

Fund of Funds. A product that invests in other funds; may layer fees.

Global Warming Potential (GWP). Compares a gas's warming impact to CO2 over a defined time horizon.

Greenhouse Gas (GHG). Heat-trapping gases (e.g., CO2 or carbon dioxide, CH4 or methane).

Greenwashing. Marketing claims that overstate environmental credentials.

Gross Domestic Product (GDP). Total market value of all goods and services produced domestically.

Gross Return. Return before all fees, costs, and taxes.

Guaranteed Investment Certificate (GIC). Deposit product with a guaranteed rate if held to maturity.

High-Water Mark. Hedge fund fee feature: performance fees only charged on new highs.

Home Equity Line of Credit (HELOC). Revolving home-equity credit line secured by your property.

High-Interest Savings Account ETF (HISA ETF). Exchange-traded fund targeting interest savings-like yields.

Inflation. General rise in prices reducing your purchasing power.

Investment Funds Institute of Canada (IFIC). Industry association for mutual fund/ETF firms.

Investment Industry Regulatory Organization (IIROC). Predecessor Self-Regulatory Organization to CIRO.

Investment Policy Statement (IPS). Written agreement defining goals, risk, asset mix, and rules for your portfolio.

Know Your Client (KYC). Requirement to collect key facts about you (goals, risk, finances).

Know Your Product (KYP). Requirement that advisors understand products they recommend.

Leverage. Using borrowed money to invest; amplifies gains and losses.

Liquidity. How quickly an asset can be sold near fair value.

Loss Aversion. Tendency to fear losses more than equal gains.

Management Expense Ratio (M.E.R.). Percentage of fund assets charged annually for management and operating costs (a.k.a. Making Everyone Rich except you.)

Management Fee. Portion of M.E.R. paid to the manager; excludes trading costs.

Market Capitalization (Market Cap). Total market value of a company's outstanding shares.

Market Timing. Attempting to move in/out of markets based on predictions.

Modern Portfolio Theory (MPT). Framework emphasizing diversification to optimize risk/return

Mutual Fund. Pooled investment vehicle priced once per day at NAV (Net Asset Value).

Net Asset Value (NAV). Per-share value of a fund's assets minus liabilities.

Nominal vs Real Return. Return before inflation versus after adjusting for inflation.

Net Profit. Profit after all expenses, interest, and taxes; the bottom line.

Net Return. Return after all fees, costs, and taxes.

Net-Zero. Target to balance emitted and removed greenhouse gases by a future date.

Old Age Security (OAS). Government pension for most Canadians age 65+.

Ombudsman for Banking Services and Investments (OBSI). Independent dispute-resolution service for banking/investment complaints.

Ontario Securities Commission (OSC). Ontario's securities regulator; CSA member.

Options. Contracts giving the right, not obligation, to buy/sell an asset at a set price.

Office of the Superintendent of Financial Institutions (OSFI). Federal prudential regulator for banks, federal insurers, and

FRPPs (Federally Regulated Pension Plans).

Passive Investing. Tracking a market index at low cost instead of trying to beat it.

Performance Fee. Fee charged on gains above a hurdle; common in hedge/private funds.

Power of Attorney (POA). Legal authority to act on someone's financial or personal matters.

Price-to-Earnings Ratio (P/E). Share price divided by earnings per share, a valuation gauge.

Probate/Estate Admin Tax. Fee/tax to validate a will and grant authority to an executor.

Prospectus. Legal disclosure document filed before public sale of securities.

Rebalancing. Bringing your portfolio back to target weights on a set schedule.

Red Flags (Fraud Screen). An indication that something bad may happen, a warning sign.

Registered Education Savings Plan (RESP). Tax-advantaged education savings plan with government grants.

Registered Retirement Income Fund (RRIF). Account used to draw income from RRSP savings in retirement.

Registered Retirement Savings Plan (RRSP). Tax-deferred savings account; contributions deductible, growth tax-deferred.

Required Rate of Return. The return needed to reach your goals given savings, time, and risk.

Regulatory Arbitrage. Steering clients or products to the least restrictive rules within a fragmented regime.

Reversion to the Mean. Extreme outcomes tend to move back toward long-run averages over time.

Risk Capacity vs Risk Tolerance. Ability (financial) vs willingness (emotional) to handle losses.

Robo-Advisor. Online platform offering automated portfolios and limited advice for a fee.

Safe Withdrawal Rate. Guideline for sustainable retirement withdrawals.

Self Regulatory Organization (SRO). A non-governmental organization that has authority to create and enforce industry standards and regulations.

Sequence-of-Returns Risk. Bad early returns near retirement that damage long-term outcomes.

Standard Deviation. Statistical measure of volatility of returns.

Suitability. Advisory requirement that recommendations fit your circumstances.

Systemic Risk. Risk that stresses spread across the financial system.

T-Bill (Treasury Bill). Short-term government security with a maturity of less than one year that pays no interest but is purchased at a discount to face value.

Tax Drag. Reduction in after-tax returns from taxable distributions and realized gains.

Tax-Free Savings Account (TFSA). Tax-free growth account: withdrawals don't affect benefits.

Tax-Loss Harvesting. Selling losers to realize losses and offset current/future gains.

This Time Is Different. Bias where investors believe current conditions break past rules—often used to justify risky bets.

Time Horizon. How long money is invested before it's needed for spending.

Total Cost Reporting (T.C.R.). Adds fund/product costs to client reports for *all-in* transparency.

Total Expense Ratio (All-in). M.E.R. + T.E.R. + other costs; your true cost of fund ownership.

Total Return. The measurement of overall change in the value of an investment including any interest, dividends, gains, or distributions minus any added investment or losses.

Tracking Error. How closely a fund follows its index; lower is better for index funds.

Trading Expense Ratio (T.E.R.) Fund's annualized trading costs as a percent of assets.

Trailer Fee. Ongoing commission paid to dealers from fund M.E.R.s.

Transfer Agent. Company handling shareholder records, dividends, and certificates.

Trusted Person. A contact you authorize your firm to reach if they suspect fraud, diminished capacity, or financial abuse.

Turnover. Percentage of a fund's holdings traded in a period; higher can mean higher costs/taxes.

Underwriting. Process where dealers bring new securities to market.

Volatility. Degree of price fluctuation; not the same as risk, but related.

Wealth Literacy. Practical know-how to build, protect, and use wealth—covering saving, investing, taxes, debt, risk, behaviour, and navigating financial products, services and representatives.

Withholding Tax. Tax withheld on cross-border payments; depends on treaties and account type.

Yield. Income as a percent of price (bonds) or dividends as a percent of price (stocks).

YTB (Yield to Broker). The invisible toll between you and your full investment returns.

Yield to Maturity (YTM). Bond's annualized return if held to maturity, assuming coupons reinvested.

Endnotes

Chapter 2

[1] Statistics Canada, "Table 36-10-0580-01 National Balance Sheet Accounts (x 1,000,000)," accessed Dec. 29, 2025, https://doi.org/10.25318/3610058001-eng

[2] Statistics Canada, "Table 36-10-0580-01 National Balance Sheet Accounts.

[3] Statistics Canada, "Table 36-10-0580-01 National Balance Sheet Accounts.

[4] Statistics Canada, "Table 36-10-0122-01 Gross domestic income, gross national income and net national income, Canada, quarterly (x 1,000,000)," accessed Dec. 29, 2025, https://doi.org/10.25318/3610012201-eng

[5] Statistics Canada, "Table 14-10-0287-01 Labour force characteristics, monthly, seasonally adjusted and trend-cycle," accessed Dec. 29, 2025, https://doi.org/10.25318/1410028701-eng

[6] Canadian Bankers Association, "Banking on a stronger, prosperous, more connected, Canada," Sept. 23, 2025, accessed Nov. 4, 2025, https://cba.ca/article/banking-on-canada

[7] Statistics Canada, "Table 14-10-0202-01 Employment by industry, annual," accessed Nov. 6, 2025, https://doi.org/10.25318/1410020201-eng

[8] Loblaw Companies Limited, 2024 Annual Report, Page 21, accessed Nov. 7, 2025, https://dis-prod.assetful.loblaw.ca/content/dam/loblaw-companies-limited/creative-assets/loblaw-ca/investor-relationsreports/annual/2024/LCL_2024_AR.pdf

[9] Loblaw Companies Limited, 2024 Annual Report, 21

[10] Royal Bank of Canada, Annual Report 2024, Page 20, accessed Nov. 7, 2025, https://www.rbc.com/investor-relations/_assets-custom/pdf/ar_2024_e.pdf

[11] Royal Bank of Canada, Annual Report 2024, Page 20.

[12] Royal Bank of Canada, Annual Report 2025, Page 242, accessed Dec. 30, 2025, https://www.rbc.com/investor-relations/_assets-custom/pdf/ar_2025_e.pdf

[13] Royal Bank of Canada, Annual Report 2025, Page 242.

[14] Royal Bank of Canada, Annual Report 2025, Pages 30, 242. Bank of Nova Scotia, Annual Report 2025, Pages 19, 128, https://www.scotiabank.com/content/dam/scotiabank/corporate/quarterly-reports/2025/q4/Annual_Report_2025_EN.pdf. TD Bank, Annual Report 2025, Pages 20, 33, https://www.td.com/content/dam/tdcom/canada/about-td/pdf/quarterly-results/2025/q4/2025-annual-report-en.pdf. Bank of Montreal, Annual Report 2025, Pages 22, 35, https://www.bmo.com/ir/archive/en/bmo_ar2025.pdf. CIBC, Annual Report 2025, Pages 17, 22 https://www.cibc.com/content/dam/ cibc-public-assets/about-cibc/investor-relations/pdfs/quarterly-results/2025/ar-25-en.pdf. National Bank, Annual Report 2025, Pages 22, 25, https://www.nbc.ca/content/dam/bnc/a-propos-de-nous/relations-investisseurs/assemblee-annuelle/2026/na-annual-report-2025.pdf. All reports accessed Dec. 30, 2025.

[15] Page 250. Government of Canada, "Canada Strong Budget 2025", Nov. 2025, accessed Dec. 28, 2025, https://budget.canada.ca/2025/report-rapport/pdf/budget-2025.pdf

Chapter 3

[16] TD Bank 2025 Simplified prospectus, accessed Nov. 15, 2025, https://www.td.com/content/dam/tdam/ca/en/pdf/tdmfspfinale-en.pdf

[17] Bank of Nova Scotia 2025 Simplified Prospectus, accessed Nov. 15, 2025, https://www.scotiafunds.com/content/dam/scotiafunds/documents/Scotia-Funds-Scotia-Wealth-Pools-Pinnacle-Portfolios-Simplified-Prospectus.pdf

Chapter 5

[18] Bryan Armour, Eugene Gorbatikov, and Maciej Kowara, Morningstar's US Active/Passive Barometer: Midyear 2025 (Morningstar Manager Research, 2025), Page 3, PDF, accessed Oct. 3, 2025, https://www.morningstar.com/content/cs_assets/v3/assets/blt9415ea4cc4157833/blt81bb25c707523e4f/6890cff4b1ec87fd0be6c50c/H2_2025_US_Active_Passive_Barometer.pdf

[19] Institute of Financial Planning and FP Canada Standards Council, 2025 Projection Assumption Guidelines, April 2025, Page 20, PDF, accessed November 7, 2025, https://www.fpcanada.ca/docs/professionalsitelibraries/standards/2025-pag—-english.pdf?sfvrsn=e15d436d_3

Chapter 6

[20] For more see "The Man Who Solved the Market: How Jim Simons Launched the Quant Revolution." Gregory Zuckerman, 2019.

[21] World Federation of Exchanges, accessed Dec. 1, 2025, https://focus.world-exchanges.org/issue/november-2025/market-statistics

Chapter 8

[22] Charles Ponzi, accessed Nov. 4, 2025, https://postalmuseum.si.edu/exhibition/behind-the-badge-case-histories-scams-and-schemes/ponzi-scheme.

[23] Federal Bureau of Investigation, "Bernie Madoff," accessed Nov. 4, 2025, https://www.fbi.gov/history/famous-cases/bernie-madoff

[24] CBC News, "Earl Jones pleads guilty in $50M fraud," January 15, 2010, accessed Nov. 6, 2025, https://www.cbc.ca/news/canada/montreal/earl-jones-pleads-guilty-in-50m-fraud-1.869778

[25] Hannah Lang, "Sam Bankman-Fried's sudden turn from white knight to detainee," Reuters, Dec. 13, 2022, accessed November 6, 2025, https://www.reuters.com/world/sam-bankman-frieds-sudden-turn-white-knight-detainee-2022-12-13/

Chapter 9

[26] Moody's Corporation, "Moody's Corporation Acquires CSI Global Education," Nov. 22, 2010, accessed Nov. 6, 2025, https://ir.moodys.com/press-releases/news-details/2010/Moodys-Corporation-Acquires-CSI-Global-Education/default.aspx

[27] Fitch Learning, "Fitch Learning Agrees to Acquire Moody's Analytics Learning Solutions and the Canadian Securities Institute," Aug. 14, 2025, accessed Nov. 6, 2025, https://fitchlearning.com/insight/fitch-learning-strategic-acquisition/

Chapter 10

[28] Fred Schwed Jr., Where Are the Customers' Yachts? Or, A Good Hard Look at Wall Street. New York: Simon and Schuster, 1940.

Chapter 11

[29] Ombudsman for Banking Services and Investments (OBSI), "How We're Regulated," accessed Nov. 6, 2025, https://www.obsi.ca/en/about-us/how-were-regulated/

[30] Commission de Surveillance du Secteur Financier (CSSF), "About the CSSF," accessed Nov. 6, 2025, https://www.cssf.lu/en/about-the-cssf

[31] Australian Securities and Investments Commission (ASIC), "Our vision and strategic priorities," accessed Nov. 6, 2025, https://www.asic.gov.au/about-asic/what-we-do/our-role/our-vision-and-strategic-priorities/

Chapter 12

[32] House of Commons (Canada), "Broadcasting Services," in House of Commons Procedure and Practice, 3rd ed., accessed Nov. 6, 2025, https://www.ourcommons.ca/procedure/procedure-and-practice-3/ch_24_2-e.html

[33] The Economist, "Leviathan stirs again," January 21, 2010, accessed Nov. 6, 2025, https://www.economist.com/briefing/2010/01/21/leviathan-stirs-again

[34] Organisation for Economic Co-operation and Development (OECD), OECD Economic Surveys: Canada 2025, May 26, 2025, accessed Nov. 6, 2025, https://www.oecd.org/en/publications/oecd-economic-surveys-canada-2025_28f9e02c-en.html

[35] Jake Fuss, Milagros Palacios, and Callum MacLeod, Caution Required When Comparing Canada's Debt to that of Other Countries, 2024 Edition (Vancouver: Fraser Institute, August 2024), PDF, accessed Nov. 6, 2025, https://www.fraserinstitute.org/sites/default/files/caution-required-when-comparing-canadas-debt-to-other-countries-2024.pdf

[36] Alexandre Laurin and William B. P. Robson, "A 'surplus' for the Public Service Pension Plan? That's not real," C.D. Howe Institute – Opinions & Editorials, Dec. 6, 2024, accessed Nov. 6, 2025, https://cdhowe.org/publication /alex-laurin-and-william-robson-surplus-public-service-pension-plan-thats-not-real/

[37] The Canadian Encyclopedia, "Income Tax in Canada," accessed Nov. 6, 2025, https://thecanadianencyclopedia.ca/en/article/income-tax

[38] Canada Pension Plan Investment Board (CPP Investments), Annual Report 2025. Page 6. "Investment Selection – Performance of the Fund against the Benchmark Portfolios" (negative 1.6% net value-added; discussion of trailing the Benchmark Portfolios), May 14, 2025, accessed Nov. 6, 2025, https://www.cppinvestments.com/wp-content/uploads/attachments/CPP-Investments-F2025-Annual-Report-English.pdf

Chapter 13

[39] Peter Lynch and John Rothchild, One Up on Wall Street: How to Use What You Already Know to Make Money in the Market (New York: Simon & Schuster, 2000).

Chapter 14

[40] A good generic indicator is the BlackRock, "iShares Core Canadian Long Term Bond Index ETF (XLB)," accessed Nov. 4, 2025, https://www.blackrock.com/ca/investors/en/products/239489/ishares-canadian-long-term-bond-index-etf

Chapter 15

[41] Encyclopaedia Britannica, "Great Smog of London," last updated Sept. 27, 2025, accessed Nov. 6, 2025, https://www.britannica.com/event/Great-Smog-of-London

[42] McKinsey Global Institute, The Net-Zero Transition: What It Would Cost, What It Could Bring (January 2022), PDF, accessed Nov. 6, 2025, page 13. https://www.mckinsey.com/~/media/mckinsey/business%20functions/sustainability/our%20insights/the%20net%20zero%20transition%20what%20it%20would%20cost%20what%20it%20could%20bring/the-net-zero-transition-what-it-would-cost-and-what-it-could-bring-final.pdf

Chapter 18

[43] Encyclopaedia Britannica, "Otto von Bismarck," last updated Sept. 11, 2025, accessed Nov. 6, 2025, https://www.britannica.com/biography/Otto-von-Bismarck

About the Author

Scott Ross is a retired Canadian stockbroker, investment advisor, and portfolio manager with a thirty-year career helping households save, invest, and make clearer decisions in a system that rarely puts them first. He began his finance career in 1992 after completing an MBA at Saint Mary's University in Halifax. Before finance, he attended Royal Military College and served in the Canadian Navy—formative years that shaped a bias toward discipline, plain-English thinking, and calm under pressure.

Over the next three decades, he built an advisory practice while navigating an industry where client's best interests and institutional incentives were often misaligned. Along the way, he earned industry-leading credentials, including **CFP, CIM, CFA, FCSI, and CIPM** (with business foundations in **BA** and **MBA**). Those letters mattered to him for what they enabled: better questions, better process, and better odds for families, not as ends in themselves.

From his vantage point inside Canada's largest institutions, Scott saw the growing disconnect between how firms measured success—revenue to the institution—and the after-fee, after-tax outcomes clients actually needed, understood, and could live with over time. In 2023, at the height of his career, he chose to step away on his own terms and subsequently wrote *Three Wolves at Your Door* to advocate for a simpler, fairer way forward.

Today, Scott focuses on practical wealth literacy: helping Canadians reduce avoidable costs, avoid behavioural pitfalls, and to hold advisors and institutions to higher standards. Scott believes investors are best served by clarity over complexity, process over prediction, and incentives that keep professionals on the client's side of the table. He continues to write, teach, and build tools that help Canadian households keep more of what they earn and invest.

www.ingramcontent.com/pod-product-compliance
Lightning Source LLC
LaVergne TN
LVHW050930210926
848482LV00013B/592
* 9 7 8 1 5 5 4 8 3 6 2 9 1 *